A Married Couple's Checklist for Having Fun, True Intimacy, and Passionate Sex, While Parenting

Getting Back to the Basics of Dating Your Spouse, Better Communication, a Strong Family Bond, and Restoring Trust

Ronni & Corey Green

© **Copyright 2021 - All rights reserved.**

The content contained within this book may not be reproduced, duplicated or transmitted without direct written permission from the author or the publisher.

Under no circumstances will any blame or legal responsibility be held against the publisher, or author, for any damages, reparation, or monetary loss due to the information contained within this book, either directly or indirectly.

Legal Notice:

This book is copyright protected. It is only for personal use. You cannot amend, distribute, sell, use, quote or paraphrase any part, or the content within this book, without the consent of the author or publisher.

Disclaimer Notice:

Please note the information contained within this document is for educational and entertainment purposes only. All effort has been executed to present accurate, up to date, reliable, complete information. No warranties of any kind are declared or implied. Readers acknowledge that the author is not engaged in the rendering of legal, financial, medical or professional advice. The content within this book has been derived from various sources. Please consult a licensed professional before attempting any techniques outlined in this book.

By reading this document, the reader agrees that under no circumstances is the author responsible for any losses, direct or indirect, that are incurred as a result of the use of the information contained within this document, including, but not limited to, errors, omissions, or inaccuracies.

Table of Contents

TABLE OF CONTENTS 5

INTRODUCTION 1

CHAPTER 1: THAT'S NOT WHAT I SAID! 7
    MARITAL COMMUNICATION 101 7
    MARS AND VENUS 10
    EFFECTIVE COMMUNICATION 13
    COMMUNICATIONS CHECKLIST 17

CHAPTER 2: IF I LET IT GO, CAN YOU BE TRUSTED? 19
    FORGIVENESS AND TRUST 19
    TWO SIDES OF A COIN 23
    CHECKLIST FOR FORGIVENESS AND BEING FORGIVEN 28

CHAPTER 3: IS IT POSSIBLE FOR US TO BE THAT INTO EACH OTHER AGAIN? 31
    AN INTIMATE SECRET 31
    A GATEWAY OF NEEDS 34
    A NEW DEPTH 38
    TRUE INTIMACY CHECKLIST 40

CHAPTER 4: I'M BORED. CAN WE HAVE SOME FUN? 43
    SPICING THE ROUTINE UP 43
    FROM BORED TO EXCITING 46
    DATE NIGHT CHECKLIST 50
        Things to do Without a Sitter 50
        Fun to Have With a Sitter Available 53

CHAPTER 5: WHAT ARE YOU THINKING ABOUT? WE'RE HAVING SEX! 57
    CONDITIONED DISTRACTIONS 57
    THE CONNECTEDNESS KEY 60
    CHECKLIST FOR CONNECTEDNESS 65

CHAPTER 6: IS HOT, PASSIONATE SEX STILL POSSIBLE FOR US? 69
    AROUSAL AND FOREPLAY 69
    THE HOLY GRAILS OF FEMALE INTENSITY 74
    THE HOLY GRAILS OF MALE INTENSITY 76

    Passionate Checklist 79

CHAPTER 7: I'M NOT ARGUING ABOUT THE KIDS! YOU HANDLE IT THEN! 81

    A Family Spiral 81
    A Singular Unit 85
    Changing the Dynamics 86
    Team Discipline Checklist 90

CHAPTER 8: LOVING PARENTS, ENJOYABLE KIDS. 91

    An Unavoidable Truth 91
    Precious Time 95
    The Playbook Checklist 100

CONCLUSION 103

REFERENCES 107

Introduction

There's nothing more precious than finding the imperfect soul who fits right into your imperfections, perfectly. The beginning of a marriage engulfs both of you with euphoric experiences, and the rush of adrenalin that courses through your bodies and minds as your souls intertwine is like no other. That is until your marriage crashes down under the weight of expected and unpredictable obstacles. Or maybe the marriage slowly but surely heads toward boredom, stagnancy, broken communication, emotional hurt, and a lack of intimacy. Just like that, what started as a beautiful, warm, and gentle flame erupts into a volcano of uncertainties. No one talks about this part of marriage. In most cases, marriage slowly becomes a negative experience if either or both spouses aren't putting their everything into the union. One spouse might feel hurt or become resentful after losing their trust in their partner.

One, or both partners don't know how to overcome the pain inside of them, but they still want to make the marriage work. They may start using unhealthy methods to tiptoe around the pain, sometimes, even pressing it down into the depths of their emotions, where it resurfaces later. What used to be slight, manageable differences that weren't a big deal, have now become major arguments that lead to long, silent treatments. At this point, the marriage carries more baggage by the day. Lines of communication start failing because the hurt spouse can't find a way to permanently resolve the feelings about what their partner did. The other spouse starts brewing feelings of their own as they can't seem to connect with their partner anymore. Both spouses feel a hint of resentment, even if they won't admit it. The breakdown in the marriage starts spreading like a virus through every part of their relationship.

A wedge grows between you, making physical and emotional intimacy as distant as can be. Sex drives plummet as both spouses fail to connect. They fail to see past each other's imperfections, even though marriage is all about two imperfect people colliding in a beautiful blend of passion. Soon enough, it becomes hard to forgive our spouses, and we may even struggle to accept forgiveness when it's offered. All the fun, closeness, and everything worthwhile in marriage starts slipping away slowly. Perhaps children enter the home, and things go further downhill from there. Suddenly, spouses are yelling at each other from the exhaustion of raising kids, driving an even bigger wedge in their marriage. It becomes a chore to parent together as the seemingly final flames of true intimacy fade away.

What both of you need to remember is that marriage doesn't have preset directions, and there will be many responsibilities both of you need to accept and provide. Most of us know that marriage is work, but are you willing to do the work is the question. It takes two imperfect souls to turn marriage into the most exciting adventure you'll live through. Indeed, it can be wonderful and fulfilling. You must know that even though marriage should be an experience you enjoy daily, boredom in marriage is common. A sign of boredom is a sexless marriage. A sexless marriage comes from a lack of intimacy, resentment, and no communication. Do you see how they're all connected? To be considered a sexless marriage, it's regarded as having 10 or fewer sexual encounters with your husband or wife over 12 months.

Shockingly, between 15 and 20% of married couples are engaged in a sexless marriage (Mauer, 2019). Another 15% of the couples surveyed did not have sex in the six months prior to the survey. So, if you're a married couple who isn't having sex at all, or if meaningful sexual encounters are sporadic, you're not alone, and this book will help you. Just a few changes can make you both fall in love all over again. Simple changes to the dynamics of your marriage, partnership, and parenting can remind both of you why you chose each other in the first place. And what makes it even better is that the changes are simple and effective. Some of the changes might return you and your spouse to the passionate, intimate state you crave. This book will help you understand and grow your marriage skills.

Learning to communicate effectively with each other can open doorways to connect on a much deeper and more enjoyable level. It's about discovering how men and women communicate differently, so there will be no more misunderstandings. Say goodbye to fruitless and meaningless arguments! Say farewell to turned backs in bed! The intimacy between you two will grow as you both learn about the needs of your spouse. If both of you desire intimacy on a deeper level, it can definitely be achieved once you are willing to understand and respect each other's needs. We often forget, as we grow in marriage, to keep it spicy. Can you remember the excitement when you first got together? Let's make it even better than that! Both of you will learn ways to heat things up for each other again, so you can enjoy each other with a passion even better than during your honeymoon period.

Spicing things up becomes simple as you mature together, and there will be plenty of excitement to enjoy along the way. You'll also learn how to give your spouse everything you have when you're alone to create a deeper connection, and you'll gain plenty of tricks to reignite the passion that once sparked your shared lives. Husbands will know how to get their wives demanding more sex, and wives will know how to turn their husbands into a compassionate and intimate partner by targeting the biological responses during sex. Either way, both of you will have mind-blowing sex again. Both of you will be enjoying sex a whole lot more because let's face it, marriage without sex is boring and dangerous. It's one reason we might consider divorce or separation.

Additionally, you'll both learn how to work as a team when it comes to the children so that arguments stop, and no love is lost between you, no matter what your kids may throw your way. You'll know how to move your family forward as one, discipline kids together, and bond as a family on a whole new level. You and your spouse will know how to balance the marriage you dreamed about, with the children you're raising, without either of you becoming overwhelmed. Both of you will be happier, physically and mentally healthier, and free from the chains that break a marriage.

We are a husband and wife team who faced many challenges in our 25 years of marriage. We're still under the age of 45, and we want to keep our marriage strong. Our experience allows us to share valuable tips and marriage advice with you.

Everybody wants their marriage to stay happy in this challenging world. We aren't strangers to the loss of passion and the hesitation to forgive, and had times where we would often discuss separation and divorce. There were times we never thought we'd make it through the storms of challenges that come with keeping a marriage strong and passionate. We also questioned whether our sex life was dead. Monotony and resentment seeped into the cracks in our marriage. We wondered whether we would ever be connected as deeply as we once were. Was it possible for us to grow deeper and closer going forward? We asked ourselves and each other many questions. Both of us knew we wanted a stronger family life, but we both had our own obstacles to overcome. They say the evidence is in the results. Today, we're closer than ever before.

We're as passionate as lustful teenagers, and we aren't shy of sharing our full selves in the bedroom. We ravish each other, and we find ways to keep it exciting, but beneath this, we communicate as married couples should. We understand each other, and we know how to let go of past hurts. It's easy to hurt someone, but it takes a special kind of spouse to own their actions, or move past a deep pain in their marriage. We also managed to find ways to improve our parenting so that it didn't affect our marriage. We wanted to be truly intimate with each other, but we also desired a closer connection as a family. Thankfully, our children are content and see a more balanced and harmonious home now. This makes parenting a little less challenging, which keeps us connected even more as a husband and wife.

We wrote this book to help other married couples find the same answers to the most complicated questions about marriage and parenting. We are not a picture-perfect couple. When a disagreement comes up, we have to consciously communicate with each other. We have learned to master the advice that we are giving you in this book, which is why we still love being in each other's presence and rush home to be together. No one has all the answers, especially when it comes to marriage, but we will share our research and methods that we used to create the marriage we desired. We promise to leave out no details. We'll even include a checklist at the end of each chapter to remind you both what needs to be done.

The checklists in each chapter will also coincide with our website where you can find even more exciting updates and spicy recommendations. You'll both be taken to a place that will make your marriage fun, spicy, and strong again! Explore life-changing products and more! Find your upgraded life as a married couple at:

www.theupgradedlife.biz

The suggestions in this book are based on a subject we're both passionate about, and we want to help you establish a better marriage. The longer you wait, the more moments pass where communication and passion can die a horrible death. This only puts your marriage at greater risk. Any minute, either of you could do something to disrupt the harmony of your marriage. Any second, either of you could say or do something that can't be unsaid or undone. For this reason, we implore you both to dive into the coming chapters with an open mind and open heart, absorbing the interesting, fun, and highly intimate details to change your marriage now!

6

Chapter 1:

That's Not What I Said!

Marriage can be the most beautiful and fulfilling part of your life. That is until one spouse says something to emotionally cut the other one, or a spouse turns their back on a conversation. There are so many ways in which marital communication can break down, and no one wants to take responsibility for it. No marriage can withstand broken lines of communication. Every time one spouse rejects another, or becomes emotionally defensive, it's like adding too much gasoline to the flames that burn between you. The flames are intended to burn passionately and gently, but gasoline changes the flames until the heat becomes intolerable. Communicating on a deeper and effective level is the first foundation of a great marriage.

Marital Communication 101

Communicating is how two people connect on a deeper level. It's how they share thoughts, feelings, goals, dreams, experiences, and intimacy. Marriage has to be a team effort, and it can't thrive unless spouses communicate their thoughts and reasoning with each other. Communication allowed your parents to teach you how to request your needs as a toddler. It's how you learned to share the thoughts in your head when you attended school. Without communication, relationships could not exist between anyone, let alone spouses. Marital communication is one of the deepest levels you'll experience during your life. Marriage takes two people and blends them into one. They must learn how to use their different thoughts and experiences, merging them together to think, move, and behave as one, or the lack of fusion will erupt into a landslide of unwanted possibilities like divorce or separation.

This is the person you chose to share your life with, so it won't work if you can't connect mentally, emotionally, and physically. Sadly, no one can read minds. Perhaps people will communicate telekinetically in a few more generations, but we're stuck with verbal and physical communication for now. Communication is a skill that can be learned. At its core, it's about connecting to your spouse with verbal, written, and physical expressions to help meet each other's needs. After all, your goals become mutual, and both of you feel the need to connect deeply. It's not always about small talk. It's about understanding your spouse's perspective, being their number one fan, and supporting them in their dreams. Spouses should be able to communicate freely, openly, and willingly, without fearing any consequences.

Marriage allows you to share your inner thoughts and feelings, as private as they may be, and this only happens if the communication feels safe and mutual. You should be comfortable enough to share positive and negative feelings or thoughts without being at each other's throats. Moreover, you should be considerate enough to not hurt your spouse intentionally. Effective communication is strategic, and it has no room for defensiveness, hurtful intentions, stonewalling, avoidance tactics, or one-sided control. It requires attentive listening while trying to understand a spouse's perspective without looking for everything wrong with it. Both spouses should feel heard and understood when the conversation ends, and they should look forward to the next chat. Fearing communication with your spouse is the first and most prevalent sign something's wrong with it.

Before diving deeper into communication, you need a reality check. This reality check is a reflection and self-evaluation, and it should be conducted by both spouses. No one's perfect, so no one's immune to doing the reflection. The first thing you need to discover is whether you're easy to communicate with. Are there underlying issues within you that hinder proper communication? Has your spouse or anyone else told you that you go from zero to 100, even when the conversation is about a neutral topic? This is a red flag because no one desires a relationship where they have to walk on eggshells daily. It takes away the comfort spouses need to feel with each other to communicate deeply. Inquire with your spouse if they're uncomfortable talking with you. This is a sure-fire way to kill the relationship from the most basic foundations, which are trust and communication.

Unregulated emotions during a conversation with your spouse can hamper the free expression of their true feelings. They won't trust you enough to share and be vulnerable because they fear further hurt and emotional damage, and they might shut down completely to avoid this. Suddenly, you have a wall between you, and this wall can grow taller with each outburst. After all, their primal instinct is to protect themselves, even from emotional outbursts. A series of unfortunate behaviors can seep into other areas of your marriage, causing a breakdown of true intimacy. In our 25 years of marriage, we have had major communication problems, and on numerous occasions, divorce and separation seemed like viable options. This happened because one spouse was unwilling to address their deeper emotional issues while the other spouse grew tired of the ups and downs.

The emotional spouse always had something negative happening. It was only when the spouse with emotional turmoil was willing to go deeper within themselves to ask the hard question about what made them that way, did the marriage enter the road to recovery. Notice how the spouse with emotional turmoil had to go deeper with themselves first before they could help the relationship, they had to want to change themselves. The direct result was that our relationship benefited from this immensely! When this happened, and the emotional spouse learned to uncover their turmoil and hindrances and practice better emotional responses, it was time for the other spouse to do some work. The spouse who shut down into protective mode also had work to do, and now had the space and motivation to do so. They also required a mental and emotional shift, and they had to retrain themselves to think and behave differently.

The protective spouse had to decide to become vulnerable again. They had to trust their spouse, and they had to give trust while believing that their spouse won't behave the same way they once did. The protective spouse had to concede that it was safe to be emotionally vulnerable again. It was a crucial and necessary step for the marriage to remain intact and move forward. It certainly takes maturity and a willing heart and mind to do the hard thing, which is to heal the connection in the marriage. If you know your family is worth you making changes for the better, then you must be willing to do the hard thing and start changing.

Mars and Venus

As much as these two planets are nothing alike, so is the way men and women communicate. Understand how your spouse communicates, and you'll already be on the right path to vulnerable, deep, and open communication. You can understand the core of how men and women communicate by looking at the research. A study published in the *Proceedings of the National Academy of Sciences*, reveals a fact that may disturb stereotypes (Nittrouer et al., 2017). It's commonly assumed that women are the talkers and men keep quiet, but this study revealed the opposite. Men talk more than women, and they prefer standing shoulder to shoulder while communicating. Men have an innate urge to own conversations, and they don't like being interrupted.

Men are more likely to spout defensive responses once they feel overwhelmed in a conversation, and this tends to happen when too much information is flying around. This is the foundation of how men communicate. Women, on the other hand, are quite different, according to professor of communications at Biola University, Tim Muehlhoff (Forrey, 2017). Women connect better in conversations that include emotional sharing. They also prefer face-to-face conversations and responsiveness or interactivity. Women feel the need to maintain harmony between themselves and their spouses while men prefer pragmatic exchanges where they can have a stance of authority. This doesn't mean men are still traditionalists, but it's biologically ingrained for men to be the head while women innately feel the urge to maintain the peace. These differences also relay themselves in the way men and women communicate.

Men prefer verbal communication while women use loads of body language, gestures, and facial expressions. Sometimes, women don't even realize how they're expressing themselves non-verbally until their spouse mentions it. Women are more likely to nod their heads, and men will listen with little body language in response. This doesn't always mean men aren't listening, so it shouldn't be misunderstood. When it comes to apologizing, women tend to lean toward humility and respect to maintain harmony, but men may feel weak if they apologize. Women tend to feel respected and listened to when their spouse apologizes, but men might see the apology as a sign of acceptance from their wives. These are the facts and they don't intend to offend anyone. Compliments are also rare with men, and they're often reserved for impressing a potential partner. Women love compliments though, because they believe it deepens the connection.

A man's mind works like the gears in a machine. They must function on facts and reason, so they won't spend too much time reviewing unnecessary information in a conversation. A woman loves getting into the details and understanding the reasons and emotions behind anything you say, so she might prefer longer, deeper conversations. A man tends to enter a conversation with a goal, but a woman will go beyond this goal to dig deeper. This explains why many men aren't great with small talk. Men will ask questions only to the point of understanding the purpose of the conversation, but women will keep asking questions, wanting to learn more, even if they already know the answers. Men prefer 'yes' or 'no' answers, but women require context and background information. Women are naturally more empathetic, so they want to know enough to truly and fully understand your perspective.

Women are also more open to share about themselves, but men prefer to remain mysterious. Believe it or not, men can also be more judgmental about new people. They use rational processing more than emotional processing, leading to faster first impressions. This can also mean they might have an impression about your conversation faster than you. Their pragmatic minds try to filter information as efficiently as possible, so they may seem dismissive or aggressive without intending it. Men also don't like being submissive. It's great that women are now as powerful and successful as any man on this earth, but men still feel innately challenged in the family unless it was predetermined for the wife to be the breadwinner and protector.

Having trouble with submissiveness can make men come across as unwilling, even when they don't want to be this way. Women tend to be negotiators who are prepared to find a happy medium for both of you as long as they're invested in the depth of your marriage. One difference couples often struggle with is that men remain pragmatic with their demands in the marriage, but women love softening their demands. Sometimes, women are too allusive with their demands. For example, women might want to be more intimate, but they don't know how to say it out loud, so they throw hints, thinking their husbands will catch onto their desires. However, men connect better to actions, and they tend to miss the hints, which could lead to underlying resentment when a woman thinks her needs are being ignored.

There's an easy way to remember how women and men communicate differently. Men prefer action, and women prefer words, even if it is just women using more body language with their verbal communication. Even though men and women communicate as similar as two unique planets, you can still find common ground to share effective and meaningful conversations. Keep in mind that a few men might be more feminine in their communications, and some women might be more masculine and pragmatic expressionists, but these guidelines cover most men and women's innate natures. The following strategies can help you both move past the differences in communication, so that both of you can benefit from a passionately intimate marriage where you grow old together.

Can you imagine growing old, sitting on a porch, and not speaking a word to each other as the crickets chirp in the background? It sounds like a boring way to live, so let's get your communication sharp enough to allow the two planets to connect deeper for a meaningful and exciting marriage.

Effective Communication

Better communication can be achieved with a few simple tricks, including active listening, better states of mind, and mutually agreed upon boundaries. The first place to start is by adopting the effective listening tool. All of us have an automated reactiveness in conversations. Everyone has flaws, and perfection is one of the biggest lies ever told. These flaws, underlying insecurities, and an inability to understand how men and women communicate can seep into our conversations when we become reactive or defensive. Anything outside of our comfort zone could make us defensive. Sometimes, we're not even being criticized, but we take things out of context. Communicating in a different way is already outside of the comfort zone, so let's be kind to ourselves and each other while we learn to effectively communicate.

However, know that this should get better once you accept the communication differences you have. It's also crucial to understand that everyone has a unique perspective, and you need to adopt effective listening to converse without negative consequences. Be honest with yourself right now. Do you actively listen to your spouse, or is your mind wandering to other places and times? Perhaps you are thinking about your response instead of really listening to understand. Avoid "by the way" conversations or communicating while either spouse is busy. Make eye contact, and face each other to help your spouse know you understand their heart. At the root of it all, you must realize they aren't your enemy, and that you share a common goal. This alone will help you focus on what's being said. Then, you can apply the four rules of effective listening.

The first rule of effective listening is that you must be present. You can't be stuck in the past, thinking about what your spouse did yesterday while they're talking about today. Listen to your spouse as though this is the only time that matters. Don't allow your defensiveness to jump into action when your spouse wants to share their concern about something you did to hurt them. Firstly, you probably did it unintentionally, and secondly, this is not the appropriate time to rehash your spouse's mistakes from last week. This conversation is for here and now, so keep your focus on the present. Pretend as though your conversation is an opportunity to learn something. Don't seek an opportunity to jump in. Wait until your spouse is finished saying what they have on their heart, and then you can follow rule number two.

Rule number two is to pause for a moment and think before you say anything or react to what was said. Ask yourself why you would want to be defensive. Is there any truth in the perspective of your spouse, and why would you react defensively to the truth? Chances are that your partner may be expressing their concerns because of something they need. It might have nothing to do with you.

Then comes rule number three, where you have to use 'I' statements to respond. 'I' statements prevent you from directing blame at your spouse for being vulnerable, and it allows you to express your perceptions, feelings, and thoughts about what they said. Avoid 'you' statements at all costs unless you want the conversation to blow up. The more you can control your defensive reactions when your spouse talks, the better they can control theirs. Use the "three I statement" rule to respond. It starts with "when I heard the mention of," which is followed by "what I thought was," and it ends with "I feel." For example, your spouse said you never listen to them. You can use the "three I statement" response after taking a breather to think before you speak.

It may sound something like this: "When I heard the mention of me not listening, what I thought was it may be wrong to use the word 'never,' and I feel saddened by such an eternal word." Not once did you accuse your spouse of anything, and so you lessen the risk of them becoming defensive. This way of responding validates your effective listening skills to your spouse, and it makes them understand how you value their perspective and feelings while you gently tell them how you feel about their statement. This allows both of you to feel heard in the conversation. Without patronizing your partner, you may ask them to share the way they feel, so that you can empathize with them.

The final rule of effective listening is to identify what you did wrong, if you hurt your partner you'll have to take responsibility for it. An authentic apology goes a long way, and it can quickly diffuse the situation while it shows your spouse how well you were listening. It's not just about hearing their words. You need to feel their side of the story, and you must take responsibility for the genuine damage you caused. No one is truly innocent in most cases. These guidelines will help you listen with a passion to resolve and move forward.

The second part of effective communication is understanding how your state of mind can change the direction of your conversation. Think of your state of mind this way: Your mind can be a runaway car, speeding down the interstate, gaining more and more speed with every passing moment of a difficult conversation. The brakes can slow you down, but they become less effective the faster you travel. So, what do you do? You gently put your foot on the brake and the car takes a few moments to come to a stop. The speeding car offers a good analogy for heated conversations. The worse the conversation gets, the less likely your brakes will work in time. Even after putting your foot on the brake, the car will still take some time to stop.

Slamming the brakes with intentional force will only roll the car, and closing your eyes when you first press the brake pedal will lead to disaster, too. It's about tapping the brake, and focusing on the road as the car slowly comes to a stop. There are a few ways you can pump the brakes, and it's best to set these boundaries with your spouse before the car speeds away in a heated conversation. Design a strategy you both can use when you require the brake pedal. You should consider when it's appropriate to push the brakes, which might be when either of you feels overwhelmed or negative. You should agree that using the brake pedal is a way for either of you to change your state of mind. The two of you should agree that it's okay to take a moment away from each other to calm down when the heat rises.

Both of you should be silent once the brake pedal is applied to the conversation. It helps to agree on a set time for this cool down period as well. Three to five minutes works well to calm the mind and give you time to think. Sometimes you may need more time, that's okay too. Once you return after the cool down period, you should discuss only the main topic that requires resolution. You don't want things heating up again. Agree on a safe word or phrase you can use to stop the discussion to change your state of mind whenever you need it. The word can be a favorite meal or it can represent the brake pedal, but it must be established as a boundary both of you must respect. Before using the safe word, touch your spouse's hand gently to remind them that this is only a temporary cool down period. Remind them of the connection you share without using words.

Help your spouse realize you're not enemies, and take a deep breath before you say your safe word, so you can say it calmly. This might help both of you calm down quicker. And whatever you do, soothe yourself during the cooling period. Don't use this time to ruminate. Rather reflect on why you feel the way you do. What makes you angry, sad, or defensive? Why do you feel this way, and is there a way you can use 'I' statements to help your spouse understand your perspective without attacking them? Add to your calmness with peaceful music or a brief meditation to guarantee a better state of mind when you return. Setting these boundaries also establishes a mutual understanding that using the brake pedal is not a free pass. It's not a method to avoid confrontation. It's also not a way to stonewall your spouse.

It's merely a tool you use to collect your emotions and thoughts before continuing your conversation. You may also not be able to continue your conversation if you have other time commitments. Reassure your spouse that this is a cooling period by setting a time and place to finish the conversation. Setting aside time for these conversations when life carries us away in a rush can also signify how much your spouse's feelings and thoughts matter to you. These tools work wonders for heated conversations, but they can also be adapted to work for regular communication. Whenever something pressing is around the corner, set aside a time and place to discuss it, whether it's about your children, career, or goals.

Use effective listening to bond deeper with your spouse by learning more about them with each conversation, and use effective communication tactics to ensure no one's toes are stepped on. We all feel passionate about certain subjects, and this can also cause emotional speeding on the interstate. Remember that your goal is to connect with your spouse. It's not to disconnect with conversations that run away from both of you.

Communications Checklist

Use this checklist in any scenario you wish to communicate effectively and deeply.

- Set aside mutually-agreeable times for discussions.

- Remove all distractions because nothing matters more than the two of you at that time.

- Write down your thoughts about the topic you want to discuss to help you stay focused on the subject.

- Listen to your spouse from a neutral place, and really hear what they're saying to you.

- Maintain eye contact during the conversation, and be present with your spouse.

- Be aware of your body language to make sure it doesn't speak for you. Only use body language to connect with a gentle touch.

- Don't interrupt your spouse, and allow each person to express their thoughts completely.

- Don't turn your back or walk away while your spouse talks.

- Don't stay away from the conversation for too long.

- Don't follow your spouse if they requested a cooling period. This breaks the mutual boundary set by both of you.

Chapter 2:

If I Let it Go, Can You be Trusted?

The second foundation of a loving, healthy, exciting, and intimate marriage is forgiveness. It must be given and received so both of you can reconcile as you build trust again. Trust is such a fragile word and concept, but a marriage without it will never flourish. Everyone stumbles, and every action leads to a reaction that affects the person we love. It's doubtful that you're reading this book unless you desire the deepest relationship with your spouse, and depth can only be supported with the foundations of a great marriage. This may be one of the toughest chapters for you, but the fact that you're here, reading this now, means you yearn to take a step toward true intimacy.

Forgiveness and Trust

There's nothing like a wedge of resentment driven between a wife and husband to complicate marriage. Imagine yourself wearing a backpack, which collects bricks of negative emotions toward your spouse. The backpack will increase in weight while the emotions are never addressed, and the time will come where the weight will be unbearable. Suddenly, the marriage goes as far south as it can. Understandably, a marriage void of forgiveness means both spouses are carrying these incredibly heavy backpacks. Life becomes a drag, marriage becomes a chore, and intimacy becomes impossible. How close can you be if both of you carry this weight over your shoulders? Even physical intimacy takes a plunge because who can make love to their spouse with the weight of the world on their back?

This weight affects your mind and heart, making you see your spouse as someone different from the person you once loved so deeply. Forgiveness is a way to start removing the bricks from the backpack. It's a slow journey that requires one spouse to forgive and the other spouse to accept the forgiveness. In some cases, both spouses need to play both roles for full reconciliation to occur. Both spouses have likely done something, big or small, that needs to be addressed. Forgiveness is to release the resentment bricks from the backpack. It's to cease all attachment to the resentment. It's a way for one spouse to pardon the transgressions of another. Forgiveness allows us to stop blaming our spouse for doing something that broke the trust, whether they did it intentionally or unintentionally.

Forgiveness is not to forget. We can't forget the event or action that took place unless someone invents a memory eraser, but we can release the negative emotions associated with it. It's the emotions that weigh you down, preventing you from being intimate with the person you married. Marriage is the closest relationship you'll ever have with another person, and you can't get close enough unless you're willing to forgive and be forgiven. Underlying resentment can cause spouses to feel in constant conflict because the act of forgiveness is but another way to resolve conflict. The reason you feel resentment is that your spouse did something that conflicts with your values and beliefs. Otherwise, you wouldn't be hurt by their actions.

The reason the transgressing spouse may feel resentful is that they also feel in conflict about why their spouse won't see their perspective. They may feel as though their actions were unintentional, provoked, or even innocently ignorant of the other spouse's values. It's common to make mistakes in a marriage without realizing how it hurts the other spouse, but it takes a brave and committed spouse to own their mistakes and be remorseful. Some couples may even sweep smaller transgressions under the rug. An example of a seemingly innocent transgression would be to invite your parents over without consulting with your spouse. You're aware they don't get along, and you may even feel doubtful as you make the call.

Your spouse arrives home late from work to find their in-laws lounging around while they wait for dinner. This transgression may even pass unnoticed for some time, and then it suddenly pops up during a disagreement about something else. This only proves how the smallest transgressions could leave a brick of resentment, weighing down on your shoulders. The problem with this is that a few minor transgressions have likely happened already, and this debate was the perfect chance to bring them all to the table. Humans tend to hoard feelings like this, and these emotions bottle up until they explode, breaking down our ability to communicate effectively. When one of the first foundations of marriage falls, the others tend to follow.

Any behavior or decision that causes emotional baggage for one spouse should be resolved as quickly as possible. Not only does it clear the air for when a difference of opinion happens, it also makes the transgressing spouse aware of their previously innocent mistake. It would be fruitless to expect our spouses to know that their behavior went against our values unless we discuss it openly and calmly with them. Sometimes, a lack of remorse simply is due to innocent ignorance. Any spouse participating in decisions and behaviors they know aren't acceptable is another story, but it also doesn't mean that they can't be forgiven.

Some of the biggest transgressions that hurt marriage are infidelity, career decisions without communication, and family decisions without seeing how a spouse feels about it. Making a huge decision without effectively communicating with your spouse is bound to burn a bridge. The good news is that bridges can be rebuilt. Research published in *The Journal of Clinical Psychology* concluded that marital quality is closely associated with forgiveness (Gordon et al., 2008). What makes this paper stand out is that it was based on married couples who survived infidelity, so it shows how we can move beyond the worst of stumbles. Increased satisfaction in a marriage required a mutual underlying desire to reconcile after a spouse did the unthinkable.

Greater commitment from both spouses, shared conflict resolution, and relationship-enhancing attributions were also noted in the research. Couples grew closer after committing to reconciliation, and they actually developed a greater ability to resolve conflicts. The couples also benefited from acknowledging how they need to enhance their relationships. Moreover, being able to forgive and receive forgiveness also proved to increase marital longevity. Reconciliation without forgiveness will run a short course. Spouses who practice forgiveness are likely to be more resilient with daily stressors, and they can express greater empathy toward their spouses. They can also communicate more effectively because their emotional regulation prevents them from being reactive, which is useful when the transgression isn't something to write home about.

Not every transgression prompts separation and divorce; otherwise, we would live in a world of divorcees. There are also differences between genders when it comes to forgiveness, according to experts (Souders, 2019). Women are more likely to forgive and move forward, but they're also more likely to be reactive because they remain more emotional. Men are less likely to forgive, but it's not an impossible feat for them. Men are also more likely to avoid conflict, which complicates forgiveness. Conflict is not the enemy. We tend to think of conflict like we do war, but it's not. Conflict is also when two people disagree on what color the bathroom should be painted before they settle for a mutually acceptable color.

Anyway, one skill both spouses should be developing and improving is the ability to see their spouse's perspective, especially when the transgression may have been genuinely innocent. This doesn't mean you'll forget because you only release the emotions. You aren't forgetting the problem, and the spouse who intends to receive forgiveness needs to remember the incident so they don't repeat it. They don't have to be reminded constantly, but they do need to take responsibility for their decisions, so they can understand what made their spouse feel the way they did. Marriage requires cooperation, and then the trust will follow. It will be hard at first, but it does get easier.

Forgiveness is an intimate response, and receiving forgiveness is a way we grow and become better spouses. Trust is delicate, and forgiveness is complicated, but these lay the foundation for so many positive ways your marriage can take a new shape.

Two Sides of a Coin

Always remember that there are two people in your marriage. One spouse cannot turn the marriage into something golden if the other spouse holds onto their resentment, frustration, disappointment, mistrust, or betrayal. This is like trying to plant a pine tree in the middle of a desert. Both spouses have to take reconciliation seriously, and both of you must make an effort to forgive and be forgiven, irrespective of the mistake.

The first side of the coin represents the spouse who feels mistrust, hurt, resentment, and offense toward the spouse who made a mistake. It doesn't help to move forward in this book until you consciously decide you're ready to forgive the person you love deeply, but who also hurt you. The door of forgiveness leads to a path that must last throughout your relationship. Forgiveness is all about regaining your trust in the person who hurt you. The part of this journey that requires daily work is where you need to trust that this person will not repeat the same behavior or decision. You must trust that they'll rid themselves of the behaviors that caused resentment in the first place. If forgiveness and dedicated change don't take place in your relationship, you may as well let go of fun, great sex, good communication, and true intimacy.

All areas of your relationship will suffer, especially sex! For the spouse who needs to forgive and let go of the hurt and resentment, it starts with a choice. This is the first step you take, albeit it might be challenging. This means you're ready to stop choosing to hold onto the negative feelings of what happened. You'll need to acknowledge with your partner your thoughts, feelings, and anything else you're holding onto in your mind, heart, and soul, to finally be free of it once and for all. You'll have to choose vulnerability and trust. You should be open and lay all your cards on the table so that your spouse can understand how their behavior affected you. And here comes the hardest part of making this choice happen, you may never know why they did what they did. Accept that you may never understand the reasons for their behavior.

The second step to forgiving your spouse is to use effective communication as a guide for your upcoming discussion. Take some time to sit down and write your thoughts, feelings, and values down on paper before you discuss them. This way, you ensure that you'll leave nothing out. This is to truly help you release the emotional hurt. To do this, you must detach your mind and heart from the feelings of what happened to you. You can't say that you forgive and that you release your mind and heart from the emotional pain, but then you bring the incident back up later in the marriage. Neither of you should ever revisit past mistakes when you feel a heated conversation boiling. That steers you away from effective communication. You must say everything you need to say, and your spouse must actively listen, and that needs to be the end of it. You won't be forgetting about the transgression that happened.

Forgiveness is not about pretending it didn't happen. It's about using forgiveness to move past the emotions surrounding the incident. You'll also have to avoid ruminating on the painful feelings in your mind. Once you have everything written down, you should use effective communication to discuss it. You will need to try your best to avoid constantly replaying the painful feelings in your mind the moment a disagreement comes up after you've aired everything out. For women especially, please be mindful that your past emotional hurts normally try to resurface the most when it's time for you to be sexually intimate with your husband because that's a very intimate time, a time that requires you to be free of negative feelings. If you struggle with this, something that could help is to focus on the here and now with your husband. Focus on your love for him and what makes him attractive to you at that particular moment.

The third step that the forgiver needs to take is to make a different choice now. Start choosing to focus on your spouse's better qualities. What made you fall head over heels for them? Start remembering the reasons why you married this person. Remember the things that make you smile when you think about them. Think about the reasons why you yearn for your spouse when you're away at work. Your spouse can't be defined by their unfavorable actions alone, because then your marriage won't last if you hold on to everything bad. Start focusing on the good things, even the small ones that make you feel closer to them. Often, the little things go unnoticed. Holding hands, a gentle kiss, a passionate night, and a passing compliment can go unnoticed after some time passes. Marriage should never grow stale like this. It's these moments that connect you deeper each time. Focusing on everything you love will slowly reconnect you.

You'll start to enjoy your partner more again. If these steps aren't working for you, and you still feel negative emotions brewing inside, there are two reminders you must consider. Building trust and forgiveness require patience. Don't expect yourself to feel like a million dollars right after the issues were resolved. It's only human to feel a slow shift back to your spouse, and you can continue using step three to remember the loving, caring, and intimate moments to speed things up. Whatever you do, don't return to rumination about the past. It still happened, but the only thing you can do in the present is allow the marriage to heal, which will happen with patience. The second reminder is that you're allowed to seek professional help if you feel unable to move past these emotions. If you feel like you need more in-depth help, seek a therapist who understands relationship reconciliation. Therapists are trained to help you navigate your emotions. Keep in mind that it shows how you still love this person if you're willing to seek therapy to heal and grow.

On the flip side of the coin, we have the spouse who must receive forgiveness. The spouse who caused the resentment, loss of trust, hurt, or offense will need to decide they're ready to open the door of accountability to get on the path of changing and staying committed to change. Your first step will be to rebuild and regain the trust of your spouse. To do this, you'll need to take the time to truly listen, understand, and accept the responsibility for the damages and pain caused by your behavior. You can't change anything unless you genuinely understand what you did wrong in the first place. You must be open to reconciliation and show true remorse, but this can only be done after you take responsibility for your actions.

This sounds harsh, but it's the only way you can move to step two. The second step for the spouse who needs to be forgiven is to work on themselves now that they understand what the consequences of the mistake were. Understand that forgiveness can't be extended to you unless you know what caused you to behave the way you did. Sit down and evaluate what you're really going through and what you can do better. Why did you assume the behavior wouldn't have the consequences it had? Where does this belief come from? Is it something you're prepared to negotiate with? You'll have to negotiate your belief surrounding the behavior if you want to reconcile. Many times, our behaviors are designed by what we think is acceptable, but our spouses may feel differently about which behaviors are acceptable in a marriage.

Identify the underlying causes of what makes you do what you do, whether it's making decisions without your spouse, or it may be as bad as infidelity. Perhaps you were raised by parents in an open marriage. Of course, this doesn't fly in a healthy marriage. Marriage is commitment. It's not a free for all buffet. Some spouses might believe it's acceptable to make life-changing decisions without their partner's input because that's the way they were raised. However, their spouse might've grown up in a home where decisions were shared between the parents. Another reason why we often justify our behaviors is that we bottled our negative emotions, thinking it's what we're supposed to do. It's what we were taught, but marriage is a shared experience. There are ways to share the emotions we must manage, and one way might be to face them in a professional context with a therapist.

Thoughts, emotions, and beliefs can lead to actions, so determine how your behaviors were designed. This is an introspection into your side of the coin. It can be hard to recognize the underlying reasons behind your actions, and it's okay to reach out to a therapist who can help you navigate this self-evaluation. You can't proceed without knowing the roots of your decisions. The third step of the spouse who needs forgiveness is to commit to a behavioral change. Write down a few ways you can change the course of your actions on a daily basis. Sometimes, you may need to challenge the perspective you've grown accustomed to. A spouse that is able to see their partner's perspective is more likely to discover ways to change their own behavior. Perhaps you can start being curious about your spouse and how they see things.

You can learn and grow by taking daily actions to find out more about the person you're spending your life with. If your mistake was to make a huge decision without your partner, you can always start including them in daily decisions about dinner, what to watch on Netflix, and what foreplay they want to lead with. Whatever your mistakes were, write down actionable, daily steps you can take to change the behavior. This can be used to reassure your spouse of your intentions to change. Your spouse will witness the changes happening daily, even if they're small things. It allows them to trust you again, knowing you're making a difference. This is so important to remember, so listen up! Your actions mean everything, and they'll determine if you can be trusted moving forward.

Change is a hard commitment, but you must be willing to commit to not hurting your spouse again. You cannot afford to slip back into old patterns and behaviors if you want to regain your spouse's trust. This will ruin your chances to have a meaningful, intimate, and enjoyable relationship. Even if you start with one simple change daily, make it count. Show your spouse how much your marriage matters to you by taking actionable steps toward improved behavior. Their trust will rekindle with time if you remain consistent in your new ways. It won't happen overnight, but you'll show them how committed you are with consistent change. A healthy marriage resembles a coin because it's very different on each side, but they have two equally important roles to play. Both spouses should strive to be empathetic, patient, and be willing to serve, to make life better for each other.

There are no heads and tails in a marriage, but there are two sides unique in their beliefs, feelings, and thoughts. This must be considered because everyone will make a mistake. Deal with mistakes immediately to avoid the consequences of emotional baggage pulling you apart. Be patient and empathize with each other as you both heal and grow through this forgiveness journey. Most importantly, take responsibility when you do something hurtful. It's the one way both of you can happily move forward as a couple. Both of you must be happy, willing, and committed to your steps toward forgiveness. If you can solidify this foundation of marriage as early as possible, you can certainly rekindle the fires that burn deep within you and be intimate, loving, and passionate again.

Checklist for Forgiveness and Being Forgiven

The journey to forgiveness in marriage lies within both of you. This is a mutual path you both must walk to ensure a good and prosperous marriage. This is the checklist for your forgiveness journey.

- Write down all the pains, hurts, and whatever feelings and thoughts you have toward your spouse. Don't leave anything out.

- Set up a time, as well as a safe, private space for the two of you to discuss the way forward. This is a very important and special time for the two of you to process and resolve what you've written down. We found some useful items when we have to be at home with the kids while needing to have deep conversations, especially for the nosy little ones. See if the items on our website can be useful to you, too. The link is at the end of the introduction.

- Remember to use effective communication and listening to understand every detail of your partner's list. Don't interrupt them, and avoid any defensive body language. Avoid an attack on your partner's heartfelt feelings and thoughts, too. Most importantly, don't walk away or check out mentally. You must respectfully and empathetically remain present for the discussion.

- Discuss ways the two of you can move forward. Create a plan of progress together that works for both of you. The plan must be realistic and acceptable for both spouses so that you can achieve a much happier relationship with each other. Put your plan in writing, and keep the plan in a place where it remains visible to both of you as a daily reminder. Commit to working toward this as a team. Find ways to celebrate the small changes and progress being made on the way to achieving your overall goals. This will draw the two of you closer and allow a chance to acknowledge and validate each other's efforts in the relationship.

Chapter 3:

Is it Possible for Us to be That Into Each Other Again?

The truth couples find hard to bear is that marriage isn't fun every moment of every day, especially when challenges need to be faced and overcome. Marriage is more than great sex, shared laughter, and open communication. There are responsibilities both spouses have that unfortunately, can create emotional distance if it's all work and no play though. From parenting to financial stability, marriage is about finding the moments in between the responsibilities, or the honeymoon period tends to fade away quickly. Being intimate is the third foundation of marriage, and it gives both spouses a way to reconnect after a long day of responsibilities. These moments remind them to light each other's fires again and keep the honeymoon period alive. In fact, the marriage will grow stronger and deeper with time if intimacy is maintained.

An Intimate Secret

The world likes to blend emotional and physical intimacy, with more emphasis on physical intimacy, but they're actually different concepts. They both lead to each other, but it's important to understand how they differ. Touch and physical closeness are ways we express physical intimacy. It's about being sensual in proximity to your spouse. It's about touching them, embracing their arms as you wrap them around your neck, and it's about kissing them as you feel that passionate rush flood your body. Physical intimacy is about making deep, passionate love to your spouse. It also doesn't even require you to touch each other. You just need to be in close enough proximity to entice and tease your partner. Sitting next to your spouse, shoulder to shoulder, while you watch a movie is also physical intimacy.

Practicing foreplay and knowing how to caress your spouse on their sensitive spot is also physical intimacy. Physical intimacy is non-verbal actions that express your feelings to your spouse. It can convey what you intend to say without words. Using sustained eye contact while you share someone's physical space also deepens your intimacy. Humans aren't only social creatures. They also deeply desire an invasion of their personal space to connect better with their spouses. Women are capable of experiencing wetness while sitting across from their husbands in a restaurant, and men can achieve hardness without touch, too. This is a simple way to understand proximate intimacy. However, there are three main ways for married couples to connect through intimacy, and the second type is intellectual intimacy.

Intellectual intimacy is when you feel closer to your spouse after having a serious conversation where you shared ideas and opinions. Healthy debating and a shared perspective in marriage are how we connect intellectually, and it can further strengthen our bonds. Planning future strategies and setting boundaries for the kids together is also a form of intellectual intimacy.

The third type of intimacy is called emotional intimacy, and it's as important as physical intimacy. Emotional intimacy is when spouses can share their innermost thoughts, feelings, and dreams without judgment because they trust each other. Sharing these feelings brings you closer together instead of creating a void. A woman may feel comfortable sharing her feelings about her body image with her husband, and a man may feel comfortable sharing his fears, which is a huge step for pragmatic people.

This is where it gets complicated because the honeymoon period is hardly a stage of your marriage where you're closest. In fact, the psychology experts at Good Therapy advise couples to gradually deepen their bond with emotional intimacy (Good Therapy, 2013). It's not a closeness that happens right after the rings go on your fingers.

Emotional intimacy is also defined as knowing your spouse's deepest desires, dreams, and fears. It's about feeling like you can see right into the window of their soul. Emotional closeness is like knowing someone as much as you know the inner child within yourself. This level of closeness doesn't happen overnight. However, some people are also afraid of intimacy, which is understandable if they suffer from the fear of abandonment and rejection, or if they struggle with interdependence.

Men are commonly independent by nature, and this can make them place barriers up, which women can then break down with physical intimacy to allow the emotional side of their husbands to come through. The other side of this conundrum is that women tend to place barriers up when their husbands avoid emotional intimacy. Emotional intimacy for women leads to physical or sexual intimacy, and physical or sexual intimacy for men leads to emotional intimacy. When you read this, you can see why some marriages don't flow easily or maintain the same accord. Interdependence becomes a struggle. A man's intimacy gateway tends to start with a touch, kiss, or orgasm. Then, they open up to emotional intimacy. Women tend to get aroused by a man who sweeps her off her feet with emotional intimacy.

Intimacy is simply another way two people connect, communicate, and interact. It makes sense why women lean toward an emotional start and men lean toward a physical start. The thing is that both parties must put their big boy and big girl pants on to put their spouse's needs before their own. This is a difficult truth to bear, but both of you must do it. It takes time to build long-term intimacy, and true intimacy may require patience, communication, and mutual understanding. Emotional intimacy requires that both spouses respect each other's needs and differences, and this will lead to closeness and a deeper love that withstands many of the responsibilities that come with marriage. At the core of it all, mutual trust, respect, and effort are required to maintain a loving and deeper marriage.

True intimacy comprises all three types of intimacy, and enhancing your marriage means you must focus on your partner's needs above your own.

A Gateway of Needs

Marriage can never deepen to the levels you yearn for if you're being self-centered. Chances are that you announced your commitment to making your spouse happy in your vows. Imagine what vows would sound like if they were selfish. "I take you to be my somewhat loved spouse, to have in the background from this day forward, through sickness I leave, for poorer I run, and I'll love you until the day I change my mind." Fortunately, vows sound nothing like this, so remember that a vow is a promise. Marriage is the most selfless relationship. It's about placing your spouse's needs before your own, and this is what creates true intimacy. Understand what your spouse needs, and you'll both be winning this game.

A woman is a gentle, emotional being who wants to be safe, secure, loved, and cherished. She desires mutual intimacy from her husband. She wants emotional and physical connections to make her feel valuable. She wants her husband to open his deepest thoughts and feelings up to her. She desires to know his fears because she wants him to feel as safe as she does. Men can be resistant to vulnerability at times, but a woman needs this closeness. She wants her husband to open the depths of his heart and let down those guards. A healthy marriage is made of a wife who understands that intimacy takes time and a husband who tries at the very least. Remember that any attempt at change is noticed by your partner if it remains consistent.

Wives don't only focus on emotional intimacy, so don't let this deter you as a husband, but allow it to motivate you to get your wife to be the woman you desire. A woman also wants to be heard. She doesn't enjoy the silent treatment or dismissive conversations. She wants you to ask questions. She wants you to dig deeper into her soul. As a wife, understand that your husband will take time to grow his active listening skills, but as a husband, it's time to become curious about the woman you married. Recognize her, appreciate her, and ask her for details about her day. This shows a wife that her husband chooses to be there when she needs him because sometimes, that's all she wants. So, read up husbands! We're about to unveil some of the secrets that will give you a sneak peak behind the inner workings of a woman.

There are a few things you need to know about your wife that will help you better understand her. She simply wants someone to lean on. Safety is the third need a wife has. Trust is a special skill between a husband and wife. It's not only about avoiding infidelity in a marriage. It's also about showing a wife how much she means to you. Sometimes, women can easily feel insecure in their roles as wives. You need to make her feel like she's the only woman who matters to you. A wife wants to be her husband's first priority, and a good wife won't take advantage of this by blaming her husband for having interests outside the marriage. A good wife will fairly balance her demands to the way her husband treats her. Make her your priority in thought, mind, and heart.

Wives also want their husbands to know and understand them. She wants her husband to study her and adapt as her needs change. Women have hormones and monthly cycles, which explains why they can change their needs from time to time. She might even like chicken today and only eat fish next month. A husband who understands the tides and adapts appropriately can reassure his wife how deeply he loves her. He will never make fun of idiosyncrasies and weaknesses, he would rather offer an emotional pillar when life gets hard. A husband should build his wife up and avoid breaking her down. Some women manage to maintain their sense of humor during hormonal tides, but most women can't.

Their minds and bodies are riding waves of emotions, and they can't always see your humor when you make a joke. Honestly, they don't need to see the funny side if you make jokes at their expense. Some husbands have a tendency to joke about a woman's weakness and changing moods. This breaks a marriage down. Never make her feel guilty or stupid. Women also love sensitive husbands who offer support, even when they don't understand what's happening. They want to be cherished, defended, consulted, and understood. Don't repeat behaviors that intentionally upset a woman. Pick up your clothes, help her wash the dishes once in a while, and do something spontaneous for her. Wives want husbands to be thoughtful. Pay attention to your wife, and recognize what makes her heart skip a beat.

Don't be the stereotype who brings flowers on typical occasions. Rather watch her, understand her needs, and listen to her deepest desires. It isn't hard to see what your wife enjoys when you spend time with her. Allow her to sleep late one morning, take her on a surprise drive alone, without the kids, and give her a massage without expecting her to be aroused. Spontaneity is great for any marriage, but one aspect a wife needs is to know her financial future is planned and secured. If you're the type of husband who typically plans and likes to get the ball rolling, include your wife in the budgets and investments plans. Women can be anxious about the future if they feel financially insecure. Share your dreams and goals with her, too. It's not all about the money. It's also about making her feel secure by including her in the direction your marriage, career, and parenting go.

Share your ideas about how the two of you can save money for college tuition, and teach her a little about the stock market if you're investing. Another form of security that deepens the intimacy for a wife is to be reminded of how masculine her husband can be. A woman wants to know her husband still wants to throw her over his shoulders after 10 years of marriage (that is if you both still have the stamina for it). She still wants to see those deep eyes, feel the power in his hands, and hear his manly voice. More than this, a wife wants to see the masculinity that resides in her husband's heart. Masculinity has nothing to do with beards, deep voices, and muscular arms. It has to do with a man's character. Exude the beast inside of you so your wife can feel secure in your life, knowing her husband protects her. A wife wants to see the man she married daily, and she wants him to show up when she needs him.

Passivity is a sign that masculinity has fallen. Be an active protector who makes your wife's knees fold. The final need a wife has is to know that her marriage is a partnership. Women need to feel as one with their husbands. They need to feel equal, even if the husband is a protector and provider. Women also have many responsibilities, which can often seep into other areas of their life, and it's common for husbands to dismiss parenting while housekeeping with an endless list of chores. Moreover, the wife might also be working full-time. A marriage partnership should involve equality in responsibilities and acknowledgments. Most wives want their husbands to lead the family to the best future, but they also want to stand side-by-side as the journey progresses. Her dreams and passions are just as important, whether she leads from home or an office. Value her dreams, and accept her as a partner.

Wives also need to understand the most basic needs of their husbands to ensure a better depth of intimacy. Men are pragmatic, and they don't have to navigate the same emotional waves that women do. This makes them simpler to satisfy, and their needs are more basic. It doesn't make their needs any less valuable or important though. Husbands need respect as the first intimacy booster. Men typically flourish when their wives believe in them. They need to know their wives trust and admire them. Husbands might not be as emotional, but they still need admiration. No spouse yearns to be with someone who doesn't admire, love, and cherish them. Being respectful to your husband is about standing up beside him when the world challenges him. Support is a two-way street in a marriage.

If you want a man to open up to you, respect him by being his pillar of strength. Make it known how much you value his passions. Share your mutual passion for his values. A man sees this as a team effort, which deepens your true intimacy. Believe it or not, husbands also want more physical intimacy from their wives, and this doesn't mean they only want sex. That's a stereotypical lie. Men want to be touched, kissed, hugged, butt-grabbed, pinched, tickled, and held tight. They want to feel the friction between your skin and theirs. Rubbing their backs after work, massaging their legs, and initiating sex is a great win for wives. It makes their husbands feel valued and intimate. They thrive on consistent foreplay, and they want their wives to kiss them like it was the first date when they arrive home. A man needs to know his wife's priority is him, just like a woman wants her husband to prioritize her.

They want to feel your sexual attraction, and they can feel rejected as a husband, protector, and partner if physical intimacy dwindles. Sex should be prioritized but so should all forms of physical embraces. Husbands also want to be seen and recognized. They want to know their wives want them in every way, which includes their intellectual and emotional sides, even if the emotional side isn't as prevalent as their wives is. They want to be affirmed and encouraged. They want their wives to root for them, and they want their wives to compliment their achievements, however big or small they might be. Moreover, they want this show of affection to be public. They want family, friends, and your children to see the connection between you. A man wants to be appreciated for all he does, and a simple "thank you" never hurts anyone. Thank your husband for being creative and romantic.

Thank him for being a great father, good kisser, and a wonderful joker when his humor isn't degrading. Keep in mind that you should also never make a joke at his expense. A man can easily be belittled, and this breaks the respect and admiration he needs. An intimate marriage requires both of you to give in to the needs of your spouse. It requires you to practice intimate boosters together, and there should be no detour from the promise you made in your vows. Allow your marriage to deepen with time, and your honeymoon period will look like a stepping stone.

A New Depth

Knowing that true intimacy requires a commitment of time and a gradual process means you both can make the effort now. Some of your spouse's needs will fall outside of your comfort zone, but ask yourself whether you want to feel your love deepen or not. Do you want to rise to a new level in your marriage, or do you want to stick to your comfort zone where intimacy may become non-existent? The way forward will connect you deeper, and it will lead to better marriage satisfaction, a mutual partnership, and the greatest sex you'll ever have.

A husband should always allow his wife to express her thoughts and feelings without judging her. He must avoid disregarding or attacking her. If she can't share her innermost thoughts and feelings with you, especially when it's about you, in her mind she won't desire physical intimacy. She won't want to open her legs or any other body part for you to be sexually intimate with her. If you want consistent, mesmerizing sex, you need to be emotionally intimate with her. If you don't become intimate this way, mental blocks and walls will build inside her mind, and she won't give you the deepest desires you can think of. These walls will prevent her from climbing over to her sexual side, and that's definitely not what you want. Assure your wife that you're truly interested in her mind and heart, and not just her body. Show her emotional intimacy by being affectionate, making sure to avoid the hotspots from time to time.

Figure One

The hotspots are called the upside-down triangle. Make an effort to avoid what lies within the triangle between your wife's breasts, buttocks, and vagina because this invasion of personal space tends to lead to sexual outcomes. You don't want your wife to think that's all you have on your mind. What starts in the front of this triangle, or at the back of the buttocks can lead directly to the vagina. Your wife is so much more than what lies within this triangle. You can still be affectionate with her by kissing her forehead, gently caressing her face, rubbing her shoulders, or touching the small of her back just above the buttocks. These are physically intimate displays of affection with an undertone of emotional intimacy because you're not trying to open her legs. These actions say so much without words. Your intimacy with her should be balanced. Allow her to make the move if she wants to. Allow her to ravish you if she desires it, but reassure her that your affection doesn't always come with expectations.

As for wives, keep in mind that physical intimacy leads to emotional connections. Notice how your husband is more open with you after experiencing an orgasm. His affection and closeness multiply as you cuddle after he has an orgasm. Physical and sexual intimacy frees his mind from wandering thoughts and frustrations. He becomes relaxed enough to go deeper with you emotionally. He won't be emotionally vulnerable with you if he's sexually frustrated. He will simply be irritated and agitated because there's no sex. Understandably, it's in his nature to desire sexual intimacy.

Wives get frustrated when they get no emotional connection, and husbands can be agitated when they receive no physical closeness. If you want your husband to be emotionally available, you must be physically available. Send him naughty pictures before he arrives, and build up to it. Use foreplay to tease him until he wants to eat you, and then make good on your promise. Never leave a man without sexual or physical intimacy. Blue balls are a genuine thing, and it causes an emotional void. The foreplay allows a wife to heat up before the physical connection, too. The bottom line is that wives should get physical for their husbands to open up to them, and husbands should be emotionally available for wives to pleasure them. True intimacy is about the both of you filling each other's physical and emotional needs. If you can both truly understand and practice this, you'll live in domestic bliss.

True Intimacy Checklist

There are a few tricks to being intimate, and some don't require much effort. We have also shared some games that promote intimacy for couples and that we like, along with other items that will make this checklist flow effortlessly. You can find them on our website at the end of the introduction.

- Make sure your spouse is adequately rested and not too tired to spend time with you. Plan to reduce the load if you know the schedule is busy, so both of you can have time for each other without wanting to fall asleep.

- Share quality time alone together by removing outside distractions like technology devices, especially smartphones. Smartphones offer handheld distractions to keep you and your spouse separated while sitting in the same room. Turn them off, and spend time with your spouse without distractions at least once a day.

- Hold each other face-to-face as you maintain eye contact. Study the lines on your spouse's face, and stare as deep into the eyes as possible. The longer you do this, the more relaxed you'll feel. Talk about anything excluding bills, kids, work, and family. This is a moment you share alone, and you should be talking about something that connects you deeper without adding stress. Focus on reconnecting and what the two of you mutually enjoy. Talk about hobbies, interests, and dreams.

- Have a ritual where you lie down in the nude together without having sex. Just talk, rub, massage, and admire each other. Do this at least once a month. This shows both of you that your intimacy and relationship go beyond sex when the clothes come off. It shows a woman that she's more than a sex object, and it shows a man that his wife admires him physically, and she wants to be with him.

- A tip for husbands is to engage in a spontaneous game. Randomly ask your wife about something she finds interesting. Ask her about a hobby or dream. Ask questions about the hobby to understand it better. Ask her how it makes her feel. The only trick to the game is to be spontaneous about your inquisitive conversations. Don't plan it. Simply pay attention to something she mentions in passing. Show her how deep you can go into a conversation.

- The spontaneous game should be played by wives, too. Randomly grab your husband's buttocks in the supermarket. Hug him like no other man exists, and kiss him passionately as you thank him for the smallest thing he did today. Share details of why you appreciate him, and massage his shoulders while you focus on something he wants to talk about. Initiate sex with him spontaneously, and allow him to fall asleep in your arms after sex.

- Have a thoughtful conversation with each other frequently. Husbands can evaluate the way their wives feel emotionally connected. Ask your wife whether she feels your support and if there's anything more you can do. Wives should check-in with their physical connection by asking their husbands if there are any additions they would like to see. Sometimes, communicating directly about both of your needs is the simplest path to thoughtful intimacy.

Chapter 4:

I'm Bored. Can We Have Some Fun?

One of the biggest challenges in marriage is when the rut happens. Couples get stuck in a rut of boring and stagnant routines. Careers require attention, children become part of your family, and before you know it, every day is painted with the same brush. Spouses carry their responsibilities of balancing home and work, and the days grow longer. Suddenly, there's a mortgage to pay, college funds to save, and the marriage takes the back burner. The rut is where married couples either drift apart or find a way to spice things up again. The former option isn't what anyone wants. It's the latter option we seek because we reminisce about the times we shared where laughter and passion were part of the daily routine. If you want to have some fun, you both need to rise from the rut and start making an effort like two teenagers again.

Spicing the Routine Up

Both of you should decide now whether you want to spice things up again or whether you're prepared to allow your marriage to become a distant cohabitation. Think back to the start of your marriage. What made the relationship exciting and fun? What made you feel passionate enough to rip your spouse's clothes off before you could even make it through the door? It's easy to pinpoint the reasons why you can't passionately tear each other apart when you enter the door if you have kids, but you can remember the reasons why you reached this state of arousal. It normally began with date night, a little flirty teasing, and shared fun or laughter. This made you both feel closer. It made you desire your spouse enough to forgo the formalities of unbuttoning shirts and taking boots off.

The animal inside of us tends to awaken when we have fun together. We must enjoy our spouses and the experiences we share to become this passionate. The University of Lincoln and the Marriage Foundation conducted a longitudinal study over 10 years, which included 10,000 married couples (Benson, 2016). This was the largest study of its kind, and the aim of it was to determine what predicted married couples staying together after the 10-year hump. Various factors were examined to ensure that the couples were equal in communication, forgiveness, and other common reasons for separation. As the couples stood on equal ground, they practiced different rituals for fun and dating. Some couples practiced weekly dates, others practiced monthly date nights, and one group didn't do date nights.

The couples who planned external date nights monthly were 14% more likely to stay together than the other groups. Weekly date night couples were also more likely to stay together than those who never planned date nights away from the kids. One result of the study was that married couples reinforced the importance of their marriage when they shared these outings. According to psychologist Kurt Smith, couples who don't invest in enjoyable, shared experiences could become roommates (Borresen, 2019). We all know how roommates tend to grow less tolerant of each other as time passes. The fun in the beginning of their cohabitation is like no other, but they quickly get sick of each other. The 10-year mark is particularly important in research because it's the official hump where couples either learn to become roommates or passionate lovers.

Maintaining a passionate attitude between a husband and wife won't happen without throwing fun and arousing experiences into the mix. You'll become bored with each other, and your sex life will fade away. The sex doesn't also always stop abruptly. It slows down over time, making it hard to notice it before it stops. Date night is largely underrated as the marriage matures, and that's why the honeymoon period fades away. Marriage will always come with mature responsibilities like raising kids, buying a home, advancing careers, and even looking after elderly parents, but the kindling fun needs to remain intact. It's also not all about sex and teasing. Remember that intimacy requires the three parts to keep things fresh and exciting. Having fun is about making your spouse love you more and more when you laugh, smile, touch their hands, and whisper sweet nothings in their ears.

It's about seeking adventure, trying new things, and spending time together to enhance your intimacy. Keeping your marriage alive with fun, naughtiness, and bonding experiences is the foundation of how you prevent the marriage from going stale. Marriage requires a blend of seriousness and silliness. Sticking to a date night routine and adding fun, excitement, and silly adventures to spice your marriage up comes with long-term benefits that deepen the connection between you. Life gets crazy, and we get swept away in the madness if we don't pause to spend regular time with each other, forgetting about the serious side of marriage. You both need to commit to making time for each other, and it should be part of your schedule. It shouldn't be left for a day when you feel like you have some energy to lie in the arms of your spouse.

It shouldn't be reserved for days when the kids are grown and independent. You can connect deeply to each other frequently by planning date nights. Intimacy can increase between you when you take a break from the stresses of daily life. Husbands might be stressed about career decisions, and wives might be stressed about the balancing act between mortgages and college funds. Take a break, be with each other, and awaken the hot lover inside of both of you to release the pressures of serious responsibilities. Passion grows along with intimacy, and you can both get back to the point of ravaging each other again. Nurturing the positive side of your relationship can also create greater resilience between you when things go a little south.

Every marriage will have challenges along the way, especially when kids are in the home. Parenting is both rewarding and complicated. Having different perspectives on careers can also challenge the two of you from time to time. The stronger your marital resilience grows, and the more passionate memories you create together, the less likely you are to succumb to negative outcomes when the two of you face a challenge.

The more fun, passion, and play you invest in your marriage, the higher the satisfaction from both of you will rise. Sometimes, we can even offer support to our partners when they face a challenge outside of marriage just by being there for them, laughing, cuddling, and making passionate love that allows them to forget about their trials. You don't even need extravagant fun to experience the positive benefits of returning to date night rituals.

If you drag yourself to bed every night, and your desire toward your partner is somehow dwindling, even in the least, it's time to shake things up. You want to arrive in bed with your desire for your spouse burning like the hottest flame. You want to crawl in next to them, being hardly capable of keeping yourself from wrapping your arms tightly around them. You want to feel energized enough to have a conversation, or make love like tomorrow won't come, and fall asleep with a smile on both your faces. Date night will also increase your playfulness, allowing you both to be silly with each other. No one can go through life on a serious note alone. Everyone needs a little spice in their soup.

From Bored to Exciting

The only time either of you should go from zero to 60 is when you're about to share in an exciting adventure, whether it's in the bedroom or at the bowling alley. Both of you must take the time to feel desired and sexy. Whether you've been together for a year, or you've been married for 25 years like us, you must continue to date your spouse. Never neglect the datable side of each other because it's vital to your relationship. It's time to awaken the naughty, passionate, and fun newlyweds inside of you both. Imagine yourselves as the young and daring adults you were when you first met. Both men and women wear many hats, and we'll be discussing one of the most important hats here for both of you.

Deep inside of every woman is a desire to be the hot lover she once was in your eyes. Women would appreciate their spouses not neglecting the fact that they're your hot lover first. Sure, they're also wives, mothers, professionals, and many other roles, but the hot lover hat comes before all the others. It's equally important for women not to neglect the hot lover inside of them. The hat must be worn, even though it will make way for other hats as the day changes and responsibilities shift. The difference between the hot lover hat and the wife hat is that the former can be fun, flirty, tempting, seductive, and spontaneous. She wants and needs to be pursued and catered to just like you most likely did when you were trying to win her over, at the beginning of your relationship.

She wants to be wooed, and she deeply desires your eyes to latch onto her as though she exudes boundless passion and sexuality. If this part of a woman is neglected and not encouraged to come out and play, then the other roles take over, causing the hot lover part of your wife to slowly fade away. Once the other hats become too dominant for a wife, stagnancy, boredom, and a lack of enthusiasm take over the marriage. The hot lover inside of your wife needs you to plan things for the both of you to do together to spice things up, preferably things she loves doing. Sometimes, all it takes is a fun, quick getaway, a dinner at a swanky new restaurant, or a new activity, even if it's not your favorite thing to do. Allowing her to have time away on her own to be relaxed and pampered as a gift can also work to rev her engines up, and it can be a treat from her loving husband.

She needs to know you love her enough to plan something just for her and that you're willing to make her life easier and more enjoyable. Doing this shows that you're thinking of ways to make her smile and make her happy. She feels valued enough for you to make an effort. She feels desired enough for you to make a fuss over her. Most women would desire a passionate and sexy marriage if the hot lover part of them was noticed and stimulated. The average woman would also love to be showered with gifts from time to time and not just on special occasions. She wants you to bring her special gifts just because you notice her hot lover side. Doing some of these things and more is the way to her heart and mind, and will attract her back to you with reignited passion. It will also help both of you experience a more fulfilling and consistent sex life.

The wife hat is the part of your spouse that has responsibilities to you and the family. This hat nurtures your emotions and cares about making life easier for both of you. The wife hat is responsible for ensuring that the home runs efficiently. The roles can be different in modern society, but some examples of the wife hat responsibilities may be to provide financially, teach the children, holiday or birthday planning, grocery shopping, meal planning or prepping, and budgeting daily expenses. The wife hat is worn when your wife takes her role as your business partner in the company of life. It's an important role, but this hat isn't too flirty, fun, sexy, or tempting. This hat can be physically or mentally draining for a wife.

Without being nurtured and catered to, a wife can become distant, have no energy, and lose her passion, and that's why you must cater to the hot lover inside of her. Ladies, just like you, men also wear numerous hats, which often go unappreciated. Most men would love for their wives to appeal to and invoke their hot lover hat. A husband would much rather stay in the hot lover hat if you appeal to it enough. If you make it easy for him to wear this hat, your marriage can seep with passion and intimacy. The hot lover hat also differs from the husband hat. The hot lover part of your husband wants you to stimulate him in different ways. You can stimulate his mind by making him think he's the best and only man in this world who can make your insides roar. He's the only man who can satisfy your every desire.

Your husband needs to be edified and treated as if he has a 12-inch penis. You must make him know how you can't get enough of him. He needs to hear from your mouth what makes him attractive to you. Men need affection too. Most men would love a long and passionate kiss, a soft stroke of the face, a rub on his back, a pat on his butt, or an unexpected grind. Men love being touched in sexual and non-sexual ways in public, too. This tickles his senses to make him want and desire your every ounce of being more. He will crave for you in new ways. And guess what? You'll both consistently have loads more fun. Men also fold when wives visually stimulate their hot lover hats. He wants to be visually turned on by his hot wife.

He would drool over you if you maintain your physical attraction. Surprise your husband with a new look on date night. Wear those sexy heels if you can, and change some colors in your make-up that will make him stare at you as if he's being with you for the first time. Spice up your wardrobe with something kinky, and try a different hairstyle to give him a completely different you that he will dream about. Invest in wigs if you don't want to cut or color your hair. Buy a new perfume that makes you irresistible as this new person joining him on date night. Drive your husband visually insane to tap into the animal inside of him, so he can daydream about what he would like to do to you as you sit at a restaurant. Play with your food as you bite your lips a little.

Give him something to awaken his inner lover. Your hot lover wants to be flirted with and seduced. Talk about keeping the passion burning bright in your relationship, which will certainly help to know what both of you desire deeply with your hot lover hats. The husband hat also has responsibilities to you and the family, as the wife hat does. The roles may once again be interchangeable in today's society, but your husband's role may be to provide financially and to figure out how to better provide financially. He should, and wants to be a protector. It's not just about protecting his family from harm. He also longs to protect you from emotional harm and stress from the outside world, which may include business, family, and friends.

Your husband may even want to protect you from himself when he's under stress. He might also be helping with household responsibilities, and he doubles as a father. In the role of wearing the husband hat, he is equally responsible as your partner in the business of life. However, if the hot lover hat is ignored, your husband could become bored, irritated, and cold. Without visual and physical stimulation, he loses interest in the marriage because he has nothing to look forward to. This is why it's so important that his hot lover hat remains a priority. As his spouse, try to keep the fun, loving, and sexy side of him alive. The hot lover hats also come with responsibilities. A husband is responsible for making his wife feel appreciated and loved without waiting for a special day to come. It's about taking her out, and giving her a night she can never forget.

A wife also needs to maintain her husband's passion by giving him a reason to want to ravish her. Keep in mind that men should also maintain their visual attraction for women. Don't let yourself go if you want your wife to jump you. Nevertheless, a wife has responsibilities to maintain a fun marriage, too. Making her husband feel like he's the king of sex also stimulates his hot lover hat. Make some noise, too, if you can. There's nothing worse than a spouse who doesn't make any sounds or facial expressions, and that goes for both of you. It extends outside of the bedroom, too. Don't just say thanks for the flowers. Say, "wow, I love these." Don't just say it was a nice dinner. Compliment your wife's cooking with passionate words to show her how much you enjoyed it.

Tease each other like newlyweds again. "Wow" and "ooh" each other verbally and expressively, but most importantly, start treating each other like you're dating again. That means it's time to start planning date nights.

Date Night Checklist

Date night plans will depend on whether you have a babysitter for the kids or whether you have to do something at home. Both ideas are doable. This is one of our favorite checklists! We have included some fun and unique items on our website at the end of the introduction to help you both create and have memorable nights ahead. Ladies, we have compiled everything in one place to help you achieve that mind-blowing look for your hubby as well.

Things to do Without a Sitter

Not having a sitter won't throw a wrench in your works if you plan accordingly. This checklist includes things you can plan while the kids are at home. The secret is to make sure everything you need is at home. Date night happens as soon as the kids are asleep. Sometimes, you'll need to plan for this if the kids are young. Have a strategy in place that tires the kids out so you can get them to bed early enough to spice things up with your spouse. Once they fall asleep, you can set mood lighting if you desire or need to do this to let your spouse know it's time now. Use these ideas for home date nights, and you can add more ideas both of you enjoy.

- Cook something new and fragrant together. Feed each other as you bite, nibble, and tease your spouse.

- Take a bubble bath together while you massage each other's shoulders as one partner spoons into the other one.

- Put some background music on to set the mood while you feed each other dessert or have a fruit and meat tray. There's nothing wrong with eating fruit off each other, either.

- You can go with a classic like watching a movie with popcorn by candlelight. Choose something you both enjoy, and cuddle on the couch.

- Have an intimate dinner in the backyard if it's warm enough.

- Set up a love tent in the backyard and stargaze together.

- Do sensual arts and crafts together. You can purchase a canvas and body paint from an adult store if you want to create an artwork while having passionate sex. Otherwise, you can also paint something together on a regular canvas. Date night doesn't have to be passionately heated. It can be used to connect emotionally, too.

- Read a romantic or erotic novel together while lying in the nude.

- Play strip poker while your favorite song plays in the background.

- Have a "first date" dinner where you both have to list five interesting things about yourself. Try to mention things that your spouse doesn't already know. You can even include stories from your childhood where you and your friends got up to no good. Pretend as though you're on a first date.

- Plan a scavenger hunt where both of you leave clues for each other to find something special. The "something special" can be anything your spouse loves. Be silly with the clues by asking them to go to the place where you kissed them down their neck. Use naughty and enticing clues to be intimate with each other, and make sure you both end up somewhere you can continue your date, whether it's at the dinner table with your spouse's favorite meal or in the bedroom where a bubble bath awaits.

- Get dressed up like never before, and roleplay a date night. You can be whoever you want, and your spouse can be whoever they want. They can imagine themselves having the biggest penis, and you can imagine yourself having huge breasts. The point is to roleplay being strangers who meet up. Perhaps one of you can play a hotel cleaner and the other one can play the guest. Really get into your characters. The wife can pretend to come into the room to clean as the guest sleeps. Then, the husband can pretend to be awake, watching the cleaner with her short skirt. Use your imagination. Roleplay can be anything, and anywhere you desire!

- Create a tasting party for the two of you by purchasing sample wines, chocolates, or whatever you enjoy.

- Cuddle close to the fire in a shared blanket, and talk about your future. Talk about the dreams you share, but avoid any stressful topics.

Fun to Have With a Sitter Available

The things you can do when you get a sitter are boundless, and it would depend mostly on the restrictions for the pandemic and social distancing. However, you should have many options that don't break social distancing in public. Here are some ideas.

- Take a dance class together or go dancing in a club. This is emotionally and physically intimate.

- Attend a concert and behave like you did when you were in college. There must be no rules about what can and can't be done to each other at the concert.

- Visit a karaoke bar. Not only is karaoke a great way to dedicate songs to each other, it's also a good laugh for both of you.

- Skating is another great idea.

- Go see a comedy show together to feel the emotional closeness again as both of you laugh.

- Don't underestimate the connection you can make in an arcade. Even adults love having fun, so nothing's stopping you from racing on children's motorbikes and trying to win teddy bears. This amplifies your silliness to give you both a break from the seriousness of marriage.

- Explore a new restaurant or a type of food you've never had.

- Go to the spa and get a couple's massage.

- Take a weekend trip to somewhere fun, light-hearted, and free from distractions. This trip is about the two of you, so don't visit family or friends.

- Have a picnic in the park.

- Go watch a movie together, and choose something where it's just the two of you, at the back. Who knows what can go down at this time?

- Drive to the nearest beach or nature reserve and take a long, slow walk to nowhere.

- Go bowling, or play laser tag, or miniature golf.

- Watch a sports game together.

- Visit a museum, and have thoughtful discussions about what each of you thinks about the art.

- Hit the go-kart track.

- Go hiking on a mountain trail.

- Do something new and scary like bungee jumping.

- Sign up for a new hobby together. This can give you weekly date night ideas.

- Start a do-it-yourself project together.

- Cuddle next to a campfire by the lake.

- Volunteer together at an animal or homeless shelter.

- Visit a planetarium to stargaze on a new level.

- Go on a cruise or visit an amusement park. Nothing is off-limits just because you're an adult now.

- Enjoy a couple's bike ride or canoe trail.

- Take the train to somewhere exciting and new.

- Start having quickies in the most random places. You don't even need to orgasm. This is about randomly being silly, adventurous, and passionate. An orgasm is allowed, but you can also simply use quickies—on trains, in theatres, and even in a restaurant bathroom—to increase your passion for when you get home. Try to have quickies in unexpected places, and don't plan it. Just do it for fun. Start being affectionate toward each other in public, and who cares about any other couple who sees your smiles as you exit the bathroom.

The list can go on forever, but there's one more secret to date night both of you should be aware of, and that is to enjoy being spontaneous!

Chapter 5:

What are You Thinking About?

We're Having Sex!

Humans have become unwilling multitaskers who try to focus on numerous things at once. This might be a great skill to master if you're a broker, yelling multiple instructions to your colleagues to keep your investments up to par, but it doesn't fly in marriage. It certainly doesn't do you any good in the bedroom. It's amazing how most people are capable of thinking about sex while they're trying to finish a project at work. They can even think about it while watching birds in the park. You would suspect that their minds would be locked onto the passionate embrace once they initiate sex with their spouse, but to their surprise, sex is the last thing on their minds during the act. It's as though our minds live in the future. As soon as we start something, we think about the next thing. So, what are you thinking about while you're having sex?

Conditioned Distractions

The only part of you that can travel through time is your mind. It doesn't matter what you're busy with now, you'll always shift your attention to the next thing you have to do. Society has become incapable of living in the present as their minds have been conditioned to travel back and forth to any place other than here and now. The reason why our minds wander off during sex is that in our society, everything is coming at you fast, and all at once. People are too accustomed to multitasking all the time as we evolved. And today, it's normal to be in front of some type of electronic device every moment of the waking day, so it is no surprise that your mind wanders off to other things when you enter the bedroom. The only thing you should be focused on is your spouse and nothing else, especially when it's time to get physical.

Sadly, you're so used to multitasking that your brain naturally seeks more information and stimuli when you engage with your spouse. It's not unusual for your mind to wander into other thoughts that have nothing to do with your spouse. In and out of the bedroom, distractions lurk around every corner of your mind. Insight therapist Noam Shpancer reviewed studies from the last few decades to understand why we're getting distracted when we're supposed to focus on our spouses (Shpancer, 2015). Believe it or not, both men and women think about non-sexual distractions just as often as they pine for sex while busy with other tasks. However, being distracted during sex can decrease the performance, satisfaction, and arousal of either partner.

Our cognitive processes are responsible for us getting aroused, how much we enjoy ourselves during sex, and the way we perform. It's a thought process that ignites our desires. Sexual arousal is highly influenced by the complexity of your distractions, which are also thought processes. The studies revealed in Shpancer's review cover the most common distractions spouses suffer from. Negative thoughts and concerns are one problem that can tug our attention away from the experience. You might fear that you're not doing it right or that you're not doing what your spouse loves. Negative thoughts are also related to a lower sex-drive in women. Women easily feel guilty about not satisfying their spouses enough, and they can suffer from body image issues, even when their spouse has never mentioned it.

The anxiety surrounding these fears can prevent arousal and satisfaction. Women may even find it hard to orgasm if they fear these common distractions. Women are mainly distracted by their appearance, but men are more concerned about their performance which also creates arousal-preventing anxiety. What makes things worse is that sexual anxiety tends to increase during each sexual encounter between you. External distractions are just as dangerous for men and women. Men tend to worry about their performance as a husband outside of the bedroom, and this can dampen their drive. Women tend to worry about the security of the family and how much their husbands desire them, which remains influenced by how they perceive themselves. These concerns, internal and external, can become negative feedback loops that are more powerful than having an ice-cold shower before trying to achieve an orgasm.

This doesn't change the fact that men still worry about bringing home the bacon and protecting their families while women worry about the way they look and whether their partners still love them enough to want sex. It's no surprise that spouses get bombarded with distractions from every corner. Women tend to feel heavily distracted if they have kids in the home, too, and men also think their wives expect every time to be the best sex they've ever had. These expectations can grow, multiply, and mutate until sex becomes an unrealistic dream or fantasy. Both husband and wife start wondering if their sex life is acceptable when they hear stories of people having incredible sex after 25 years of marriage. Indeed, it's possible and sustainable to have great sex for the rest of your marriage, but expecting every time to be something exceptional is setting yourselves up for failure and disappointment.

The best way to experience sex fully and completely each time is to remain present and mindful of your body and thoughts. Stop thinking about the to-do list you never finished. Stop worrying about whether your wife thinks you're attractive. She wouldn't have married you if she wasn't attracted to you. Don't give in to the fears that tomorrow brings around finances and college funds, either. There's nothing you can do right now as you lie next to your husband or wife in bed. You can't run to the casino and miraculously win a million dollars to settle your finances, but you can enjoy the moment you have right here and now. Then, you may feel fresh enough to focus on the concerns of tomorrow. Mindfulness is a great tool to use in marriage, and especially in sex.

Mindfulness is about being present for every moment, and sensation of the experience you're sharing right now. You can't reach an orgasm unless you pay attention to your body and the sensations flowing through your pleasure centers. You have to be with your spouse to enjoy them. You can't do this if your mind wanders to another place and time while you're robotically moving back and forth. You have to show your partner how this connectedness courses through you as you try different positions and tricks. Another great thing mindfulness teaches us is that we have to be aware of everything happening to, and around us, in the present moment without being judgmental. You can't be judgmental to yourself, your body, or your performance.

You can only flow with the experience as it unfolds, and allow the sensations to move you closer to a more intimate place where an orgasm will erupt through you. And whatever you do, don't expect what might not happen. Don't expect to enjoy something new you try. Don't expect your spouse to be better every time, and don't expect yourself to orgasm in two minutes because you're in a rush. Sex should never be rushed unless you're having a quickie before work. Sex should be a sensually complete experience where both of you get lost in each other's present moments. Great sex is a journey, not a destination. What cums will come—pun intended. The distractions have to fall away before you can truly connect deeply during sex and experience every unimaginable moment between you.

The Connectedness Key

Sex is a doorway to helping both of you connect on a deeper level and be more intimate with each other. Intimacy requires emotional bondage, but it can't lack physical connection in a marriage. Most married couples desire an intimate connection during sex, but they find it hard to move past the technicalities or details of sex itself. Sex becomes a chore when you worry about details like whether you're doing it right or if your spouse feels as connected to you as you do to them. The anxiety about these details can place a wedge between your connectedness and the pursuit of pleasure. There's nothing wrong with a heated quickie in the back of a car, but to truly connect on the deepest level with your partner, you need to be making love to him or her as though they're your best friend. This is not a one-night stand.

Marriage is about maintaining the connection in the long run. Failure to connect during sex will prevent you from sharing openly with each other. Being best friends is the first stepping stone. Best friends are connected emotionally, mentally, and physically. Another way to improve your focus on each other in the present is to start setting the stage before having sex. Moods don't always change instantly, and you might need to make an effort to bring your spouse's mind to the present, to you. Choose times to have sex where you can't be disturbed by kids, phone calls, or runaway thoughts. Quickies should be reserved for heated moments before work and when you both feel like the rush that comes from the risk of being caught, but the stage for deeply connected sex must have no interruptions to steal your attention away from each other.

This means you might have to send the kids to grandma's for the night, and you may have to switch your phone off while focusing on your spouse. You can add some sensual music and light some candles to set the stage. Don't omit foreplay when you're building up to your most intimate time. Tease your spouse during the day when you both know sex is on the table tonight. Send them naughty images at work, and whisper into their ears what you intend to do to them when they get home. Touch your spouse in ways you know makes them hot. You want to connect emotionally before sex, too. Provoke the animal inside of your spouse with gentle embraces when they least expect it. Give them a naughty look from across the room, and grind yourself against them when you hug them. You need to become intertwined during sex, and not only in the physical sense.

Having sex as best friends removes the fears of technical details and judgment. It's just you and your best friend, who's also your husband or wife. You'll both be able to surrender yourself fully in the bedroom when you reach the closeness of best friends who both want to keep things spicy to avoid boredom and stagnancy. Remember when you first started having sex. Would you ever have thought sex could become a boring chore? No, you would never have imagined this, but it happens when couples lose connectedness and a mutual desire to try new things. Both of you should be focusing on improving your connectedness during sex. Grow comfortable with your body if you struggle with body image issues. Spend time getting to know yourself and the areas of your body that tingle with excitement. Take care of your body to the best of your ability.

Self-care is a sure-fire way of showing your spouse how much you value sex. Getting to know your body better is a great precursor to sharing your insights with your spouse. Talking about sex and what both of you like or dislike is something healthily married couples do. No one should expect their partners to know what they love and hate, unless they speak up. The two of you should also clear the air before having sex, or the underlying emotions and thoughts will come to the surface while you're trying to connect with your spouse. Don't leave it be if your husband said something to hurt you. Don't leave your wife be if she made you feel like less of a man today. Speak up, and allow the negative emotions and thoughts to dissipate before having sex. Resentment and other negative feelings can bottle up, until you notice how your sex life suffers.

Get it out there. Best friends talk things through. They connect emotionally before they get physical. Another way couples often struggle to connect deeply is when sex becomes monotonous. It's the same routine every time, and nothing ever shakes up the way you connect to each other. We get into routines because it makes us feel safe with our spouses. The truth is that most people have fantasies they'd love to explore. Exploring them would require both of you to step away from the comfort zone. What's the worst that could happen when you try something new? You could both dislike it, but you'll never know if you would like or dislike it unless you try it. Try new techniques and positions. You both might find something that works better until you shake it up again. Monotony doesn't allow for openness and vulnerability, which are both required to connect emotionally during sex.

Besides, every couple has some incompatibilities, which brings forth another reason why couples struggle to connect. Focusing on your spouse's imperfections will prevent you from connecting deeper. You shouldn't be focused on your or your spouse's imperfections. What happens with two perfectly similar puzzle pieces? They don't fit into each other. They don't hold onto each other. Both of you are unique puzzle pieces who should complement each other. Sex also needs to be prioritized as a tool to connect deeper with each other. Being erotically connected to someone reinforces how we differentiate the married relationship from others. Sex will never be viewed as a chore when both spouses learn to find their connectedness and prioritize the intimate ritual. Newlyweds often have a lustful sex drive, and they don't realize how they must shift to intentional sex once the heat drops a little.

As marriage matures, maintenance sex is one of the key factors to connecting spouses in the long run. Both wife and husband need to understand that a marriage can't thrive unless all forms of intimacy are maintained. Sure, the days will come where a wife might not be turned on as much as her husband is, or maybe the husband isn't as hard as his wife wants him to be. This doesn't mean the husband and wife aren't into each other. They merely need to dedicate their focus to enjoying the experience as it unfolds. Sex is a journey, remember? It's not about reaching a specific destination, such as an orgasm. It's about enjoying every sensual feeling inside your body and mind while you're engaged with your spouse. An orgasm is merely an end, but being deeply connected during sex can make the entire experience as orgasmic as you can imagine. Don't allow yourself to be concerned about performance.

If you're focused on the here and now of the experience, you might succumb to micro-orgasms throughout the journey. Being present allows you to be aware of every tiny change in your body, genitals, and mind. Surrender yourself completely to the sacredness of the experience as a journey. This would connect both of you in a new way because your outcome isn't the only desirable bond you share. You're also sharing every second of the journey from here to there. Both of your bodies can share an experience so deep that you'll get lost in it, but just to be clear, sex is mostly about what's going on in your mind and not your body. The deeper the connection is during sex, the more explosive your orgasm can be. Don't fall into the trap of unrealistic expectations though.

Sex between the two of you doesn't always have to be a tremendous production for it to be truly memorable, blissful, and mind-blowing. Sex is all about the connection between you during the experience. Some women may have a hard time staying focused during sex, especially if there are young children in the home, or if she never finished her to-do list for the day. Some men may struggle to focus on their wives because they're trying their best not to orgasm too soon. They think of everything and anything to delay the orgasm, which can unintentionally turn them off again. For some men, being connected during sex can be situational. For example, if things are good in your relationship and finances aren't an issue, a husband is more focused on his wife while having sex. If the relationship and finances aren't looking good, he could be thinking about other women or anything else during sex.

His main goal in this state of mind could be to have an orgasm and nothing else. He isn't connected deeper to his partner, and he's turning the journey into a destination again. Both of you need to connect mentally and not just physically. This will take time, and you both need to be and stay present in your conversations, date nights, and during sex. Keep a strong connection between you in everything you do together, especially sex. This means more touching, rubbing, talking, and whatever else stimulates the both of you. Connect deeper with your spouse by touching them in ways that aren't only sexual. Gently stroke their arms during sex, or run your hands through their hair. Make your spouse feel like you're only focused on them by making an emotional connection during sex. Talk to them while you're having sex, too. But don't talk about things that make your spouse focus on anything but the experience.

You can talk dirty to each other. Make your fantasies known to your spouse as you squirm under them. Pause your motions for a moment, and tell your spouse what you love about the technique they're using. Hold their face in your hands as you ask them for more. Tell your spouse how close you feel to them right now and how you wish you could be this close every moment of the day. When talking dirty, be as detailed as you want. Paint a picture in your spouse's mind as you make love to them. Share your fantasies to bring your spouse's attention back to the here and now, which also brings your focus to what you're doing right now. Connecting sexually will take your relationship to a whole new level, and you can encourage the connection by focusing intently on your spouse. Both spouses should be as focused and involved in sex as possible to make a deeper connection.

Stop worrying about tomorrow and thinking about yesterday. Engage fully with the person in front of you (or behind). Your bodies are complementing each other, fitting into each other like jigsaw puzzle pieces. Every movement, touch, and kiss are intertwining your minds, bodies, and souls into one. The body might be doing the work, but it's the mind unveiling the pleasures within the exercise. It's the mind releasing hormones that connect you deeper to each other. It's the mind that needs to stay focused on your spouse. That way, the body and soul will follow, allowing you to feel pleasure in the experience. Pleasure isn't reserved for the end or the orgasm. It's about enjoying every moment between foreplay and the orgasm, while hoping to end the erotic session with a mutual reward.

Checklist for Connectedness

Connecting to each other on the level happily married couples require is about combining emotional and physical intimacy in the moment. Focusing on your spouse might not come naturally at first. You both may require some practice, and that's fine. Practicing sex can be an exciting experience on its own. This checklist should help both of you engage with your partners in a new way.

- Intentional focus requires practice, so you can both train your minds to intentionally focus on a single task without multitasking through mindfulness. Start practicing daily mindfulness by training yourself to pay attention to a single task or experience. It doesn't have to be practiced during sex. You can train while you listen to mindfulness meditations, or by being mindfully present at a quiet and romantic dinner with your spouse. One way to train the mind is to experience the dinner in full, with all five of your senses. Practice this during your dinner. Focus on the way your spouse talks, the movements of their mouth, and touch their hands gently. Start implementing the same trick during sex. Use your senses to bring your awareness to the present so you can both focus on each other without outside distractions.

- Apply foreplay, foreplay, and more foreplay to your relationship. It can start hours before you have sex. Play with each other mindfully. Learn to focus on how it feels when you tickle your husband's back gently. Focus on how it feels when you grind yourself against your wife as she stands in the kitchen. There can never be enough foreplay in a marriage. It helps both of you be present when you get to the bedroom because you've teased each other enough to not be able to think of anything else.

- If you were to use science to connect deeper, you should be maintaining eye contact during sex, too. It might be uncomfortable when you try it at first, but looking deep into the soul and desires of your spouse can ignite a deeper experience. You'll be looking straight into the window of your spouse's most passionate being, and you'll maintain your focus on them. A study published in *Psychological Science* revealed the benefits of eye contact during sex (Bolmont et al., 2014). Couples who maintain eye contact successfully experience heightened feelings of love, general affection toward their partners, and deeper passion during sex. The benefits are worth the effort of trying to maintain eye contact, even if it feels weird at first. Eye contact is a valuable part of emotional intimacy, so it makes sense that it promotes a deeper connection during sex. Eye contact can make you both feel vulnerable, and it encourages trust.

- Kissing during sex is another underrated necessity for married couples. You should be kissing a lot more during sex. Passionate kissing has numerous benefits for your connectedness during sex (Santos-Longhurst, 2018). Your happy hormones are elevated, such as serotonin and dopamine, making the simple act of kissing as effective as a drug. Stress hormones like cortisol are decreased, and oxytocin, which is the hormone that bonds us deeper to others, is also released in abundance. The longer you kiss, the more oxytocin you experience. Oxytocin lights up your pleasure centers and makes you feel closer to your spouse. The decrease of stress hormones can make you feel more confident, and it can combat a lack of self-esteem in the bedroom. Anxiety is no match for your attention when you're being flooded with bonding hormones. Moreover, kissing can boost your arousal if you're not feeling up to sex. Testosterone is a chemical released by men when they kiss women, and the longer you kiss, the more testosterone enters a woman's system. Testosterone is a sex-driving chemical machine. You'll both be hot as hell in no time.

Chapter 6:

Is Hot, Passionate Sex Still Possible for Us?

Now that you know how to connect deeper with your spouse during sex, it's time to turn the heat up so both of you can find euphoric moments and experiences. The best way to make sex an unforgettable and unimaginable experience is to know what differs between male and female sex drives, and how to amplify each so that both of you get the fullest experience. Biologically, there's a reason why men and women differ in sex. Understanding the details of this will help you both meet your spousal responsibilities in the bedroom. When we say responsibilities, we don't mean it as a chore. We mean responsibilities as in how you can both turn sex back into a hot and passionate experience between a husband and wife because yes, it's possible.

Arousal and Foreplay

Foreplay is already mentioned as a way to connect two people deeper in an intimate way, but it's also the forerunner for arousal and optimal pleasure. A fun, passionate sex life doesn't just happen by fluke. It happens by intentional design. The two of you must take the time to create it. There will be quickies, and plenty of them, hopefully. However, to have the passionate "I can't stop thinking about you or what we did" episodes, that only comes when setting time aside for foreplay and arousal. This is a step that shouldn't be skipped, most of the time. Please understand this. Just because you're wet or hard doesn't mean you're truly aroused and mentally ready for sexual intimacy. Having sex without proper arousal will lead to both of you being disappointed and unsatisfied.

Foreplay is a collection of mental, physical, and emotional acts shared between two people before engaging in sex. Foreplay intends to activate and enhance arousal. There's no precise way to initiate guaranteed foreplay between two unique spouses. Every woman and man loves their buttons pressed in different ways. What complicates it more is that the buttons, or their order, aren't even the same from day to day. That's why changing things up certainly keeps a marriage alive. Foreplay is the precursor to the main act, sex. It allows a woman's inhibitions to fall, and it gets her willing and excited to receive her husband. According to the Boston Medical Group (2018), foreplay for women is the difference between enjoyable and painful penetration.

A woman's clitoris gets harder, and her cervix rises to make space for your penis. The vagina also becomes properly lubricated to avoid any friction, tears, or discomfort. Once your wife is ready to receive you, she'll enjoy the penetration more, and you'll also benefit from reduced friction and discomfort while moving in and out of her. Most women require the building crescendo, or they won't reach an orgasm. One thing both of you should put out in the open and discuss honestly, is making sure wifey is having orgasms when you have vaginal sex. Also, make sure her orgasms are pleasurable. Sex won't appeal to a wife if she's not happy in this regard. So, start discussing this now before assumptions are made and the two of you grow unnecessarily distant. Not discussing something this intimate can certainly drive you apart.

Foreplay is considered the holy grail for women to reach better orgasms. Not surprisingly, men also enhance their experience and orgasm by playing around before sex. Men are more easily stimulated and aroused by visual foreplay, but women are more likely to be aroused properly if you target the brain. Women also require more foreplay and arousal than men do. Women aren't always turned on with a simple sneak peek of your buttocks when you get out of the shower. She has so much on her mind distracting her from the visual stimulation. Men, on the other hand, can be turned on by this stimulus, but they also could use additional foreplay to make the experience otherworldly. With better blood flow allowing your penis to be properly erect, and with enough lubrication to make penetration more comfortable and enjoyable for both of you, foreplay is a must.

A husband's chances of helping his wife reach orgasm are also heightened during foreplay. Most women have an advantage that comes harder to men, they can achieve multiple orgasms. Men can also reach multiple orgasms too, but it requires more work and focus. Reaching into a woman's brain to stimulate her seems complicated as well, but it's not once you find a few tricks that work. Just remember to change your tricks from time to time, and the two of you should be discussing what works for both of you. Wives should be stimulating their husbands for better arousal and orgasms, too. The bottom line is that failure to stimulate and arouse a woman enough can lead to her resentment for sex. Women who don't experience proper arousal, pleasure, or orgasms during sex eventually lose their desire for it. It's not to say men can't lose desire, either.

Research published by Doctor Nor Ashikin Mokhtar helps us understand how hormones play a role in sex for men and women (Mokhtar, 2012). Arousal and pleasure start with a desire. The brain is where all the wonders of sex start and end. Desire is ignited by an attraction, which is a chemical fluctuation of noradrenaline, dopamine, and catecholamines. Testosterone and another chemical called dehydroepiandrosterone or DHEA also rise when you feel desirably attracted to your spouse. Serotonin is also released in the brain to ignite the erection of the nipples, the penis, and the clitoris. Your body does something amazing while you're feeling hot and trying to ignite arousal in your partner through foreplay.

The brain releases a hormone called pheromones, which increase with your desire. Pheromones are then smelled by your spouse, which activates their desire. Once a woman becomes aroused, her body starts releasing estrogen, which ignites even more pheromones. Both of you are excreting pheromones at this point, and it allows your spouse to increase their hormonal levels while smelling your sexual scent. Every hormone in men's and women's bodies works on a feedback loop. The feedback will either cause more production or slow it down. The longer you enjoy foreplay together, the more pheromones, estrogen, and testosterone are entering your bloodstream. Saliva, vaginal fluids, and blood flow to the clitoris increase more and more, and men experience better blood flow to the penis area.

The stress hormone, cortisol, is also released, but it has a function in sex. It increases your heart rate and prepares the body for higher energy consumption. As the heart rate grows, so does the blood flow increase. Growth hormones multiply, making it easier to maintain the erect clitoris or penis. As both of your bodies reach nearer to the climax of your experience after penetration, noradrenaline is released to allow your body to abruptly respond to an unexpected reaction, which we simply know as an orgasm. The adrenaline flowing through your system is responsible for ejaculation in the case of men, and orgasm in the case of women. Oxytocin levels also increase, and a woman's pelvic region contracts while she feels the after-effect of an orgasm.

There's one more important chemical response that both of you should know in case either of you complains that your spouse falls asleep after sex. Progesterone is released after an orgasm to help the body relax deeply, which can make your spouse feel drowsy. Women also tend to release more progesterone than men, making them even more passive after an orgasm. The deep sleep hormone called melatonin is also released, making you feel even sleepier. So, don't think your partner is being rude if you find them drifting off after sex.

Sexual desire in men is proven to be higher than in women, and this also needs to be acknowledged by both of you. According to Neuropsychiatrist and author Louann Brizendine who wrote *The Male Brain*, a man's sexual desire, hidden within the hypothalamus, is two and a half times the size of that in a woman (ABC News, 2010). From the teenage years, the male desire to be sexual and physical is more than twice as large in the brain as it is in female brains. This also means that men have more than twice the amount of testosterone in their brains. Brizendine also found that men tend to rely on their analytical minds, but women are driven mostly by the amygdala, which is a small gland in the middle of the brain, and it's highly emotional. Knowing how the amygdala and the female brain works, Brizendine recommends that foreplay starts 24 hours before sexual engagement. The amygdala doesn't like letting things go, so it holds onto and builds upon the memory for 24 hours, which can be used to increase your wife's arousal over an extended period until she can't keep her mind off of you anymore.

Just the same, the amygdala will also hold onto negative emotions for 24 hours, so your wife might feel negative toward you when you're hot and ready to start foreplay if you argue within that period. Keep this in mind, and allow your wife the extended foreplay to break down her emotional attachment to the negative feelings. Everything that happens in a woman's life stays within her emotional region for 24 hours, which can also benefit her if she experiences mind-blowing sex. One way to break through this emotional hold over her mind is to hit her with foreplay tactics, such as showering her with thoughtful gifts earlier in the day, massaging, kissing, hugging, grabbing, and whispering things she likes into her ears. Oxytocin breaks the barrier, and it can help your wife become aroused enough for both of you to enjoy every second of your lovemaking.

Husbands should hone into the incredible powers of the mind and the hormones that lead to exponentially intense arousal. Wives shouldn't think men don't want foreplay, either. The hormonal multiplication allows your husband to experience mind-blowing sex versus a quickie in the stairwell. At the end of the day, passionate and hot sex leads to an improved connection and better intimacy between you. Foreplay is definitely overlooked, but it's what builds desire and intensity for both of you. Foreplay and arousal should be an all-day affair of back and forth teasing and intimacy. It's all about setting the tone for an unforgettable experience, so when you have the time for sex, it's a blissful, potent, and intense pleasure for both of you. Relaxing the body by using biology and hormonal hacks right before sex can be one way for you to increase the intensity of your lovemaking.

Foreplay can be a massage in a hot bath without touching each other's hot spots. Foreplay means you need to hold out a little to create intensive momentum. If you do this correctly, your spouse will beg for penetration, or entry for sure.

The Holy Grails of Female Intensity

Some tricks, and foreplay, can make a woman go mad. You'll have your wife squealing with pleasure if you drive her desire and arousal up the walls. Some tricks can be used by you as the husband, or your wife can engage herself in arousal while she waits for your return home. A wife can make her engines hum by exercising, which increases blood flow to her genitals. She also gets the doubled benefit of feeling competitive. Women who anticipate competition can experience a boost of testosterone. Heat also boosts the blood flow to the genitals, and that's what makes those hot bubble baths so precious. Try having a hot bath before having sex, or you can place a warm cloth over your vagina to get the blood flowing better in the region. Wives should also pay attention to pre-stimulation with vibrators. Husbands can join in the fun, or wives can get their juices flowing before he arrives.

You can even get the vibrating bullets you can insert into your vagina while you're having dinner at a restaurant. The vibrations from the bullet will stimulate the muscles in the pelvic area, and no one will be the wiser. Make an effort to touch your husband gently every time you feel a rush of sexual hormones, which will happen when you're sitting discreetly with a bullet. The intensity of sex will explode after such a naughty dinner. There's something about being naughty in public that further intensifies the experience. You can also purchase a teledildonic, which is a remotely activated bullet vibrator that allows your husband to activate it while he's at work. Sexual toys have evolved from the dark ages of scary vibrators with stubs and ridges. Any woman you see could be sitting on a bullet, sexting with her husband as he activates the device remotely.

Men can even get a matching device called a vibrating ring that's activated by you as you guys tease each other from a distance. Many of the modern sex toys also carry memory cards, which allows the device to store preferred settings. These preferences can also be fed back to your spouse so they know what you like when they get to you. As a wife, you should want to find your accelerators so you can share them with your husband. You should gently take his hand while you kiss him, and move it toward the spot you like during foreplay. Your husband won't know where your sensitive spot is unless you show him. Sometimes, you'll have to figure this out for yourself. It's about getting in touch with your body so you can guide your husband when you're together.

Another toy you can consider if you want to target the infamous G-spot and clitoris together is a dual wand. And just to be clear, these toys aren't reserved for foreplay. You can even have sex while using them, but make sure you're focused on your husband. Allow your husband to make you orgasm. Don't give in to the toys if you're using them while you're engaged with your husband. He must make you orgasm for the both of you to enjoy the experience. However, let's take a few steps back again. Another exercise you should be practicing at home as a wife is Kegels.

Kegels are when you intentionally pull the pelvic muscles tight and release them. Do at least 20 Kegels daily so you're controlling your pelvic region during and after foreplay. You'll learn to relax your pelvic muscles at will during future foreplay. A secret with the Kegel is to practice it while your husband is inside you, too. Men love feeling pelvic muscle contractions while having sex. It stimulates their nerve endings without you moving back and forth. Don't be afraid to ask for more foreplay, either. Your husband wants you to tell him what you desire. He wants you to be aroused so both of you can enjoy more intense sex. Push yourself to be a little naughty by initiating arousal. Send him a text when you know he's in an important meeting. Kiss him while you grind against his aroused penis as he walks into the door. Call him when he's playing golf, and talk dirty to him.

You'll be surprised how much you can stimulate yourself when you become more demanding. Being passive doesn't always get you both pumped. Sometimes, you need to demand what you want. Call him and say, "Honey, I'm about to mindfully masturbate, and I'm going to wait for you while you rush back." Be naughty and take charge. There are no limits, and your husbands' pheromones will kick yours up when you both show an increased desire. Embrace a deeper connection with your husband during foreplay with the eye gazing tantric technique, too. Sit facing each other as you gaze deeply into your spouse's left eye. Staring at the left eye allows you to focus on your gaze and not which eye to look at. Increasing your connectedness already allows the sex hormones to thrive between you. The two of you can also try new rhythms to increase your arousal.

The coital alignment technique is when your husband lies on top of you, lining his pelvis up with yours. Now, push yourself upward and forward to allow your clitoris to touch the base of his penis as you rock back and forth gently with your legs wrapped around his thighs. You don't even have to penetrate at first. This is like dry-humping in the nude. Once you engage in penetration, and you're making love, try to focus on your experience again. Allow yourself to reach near an orgasm, and then stop so you can build it again. The second time around will be even more intense. This is called edging, and it can be used by both of you. Finally, wives can target the optimal time of the month to strike an initiation of arousal with their spouses. Foreplay increases your arousal at certain times of the month and day.

Men become more sensitive to the sexual hormones in the early mornings when their testosterone is off the charts, but women are more easily aroused in the afternoons and over weekends. Moreover, women have two days of optimal desire available every month. The first two days of a 28-day cycle are when a woman is highly sensitive. Her clitoris is harder, she gets easily wet, and she's likely to warm up to her husband faster, making sex more enjoyable for both of them. These tricks should help both of you design a better foreplay strategy for the wife, but men also deserve some boosters to increase their intensity.

The Holy Grails of Male Intensity

Orgasms are more easily experienced by men, but many husbands would love more intense orgasms. Who wouldn't though? These tricks will amplify arousal for a man, and they can be initiated by the husband or wife in most cases. A husband also deserves a toe-curling experience as much as his wife does, so increasing a husband's intensity is just as vital if sex is to be enjoyed by both spouses. The first way men can increase their intensity during sex is to practice Kegels as their wives do. Men also have a pelvis, and controlling the contractions within the pelvis can amplify the intensity of orgasm during sex. Practice Kegels by contracting your pelvic muscles as though you're stopping a stream of urine midstream. You can also watch your penis move up and down if you have an erection.

The Kegels will also help you achieve the squeeze technique if you want to edge your orgasms. Orgasms and ejaculation are different things. You can experience an orgasm or as close to one as possible without ejaculating. Ejaculation will cut most men's sexual desire down as they experience the relaxing hormones that follow, but edging your orgasms can help you even experience multiple orgasms or micro-orgasms. Once you've exercised your pelvic muscles, you can use your thumb and index fingers to squeeze the bottom of your shaft as you're about to climax. This prevents you from ejaculating. You can also purchase a penis ring to stop the flow of ejaculation, which has a second benefit. A cock ring prevents the blood from leaving your penis so you can maintain an erection for longer.

Your erection will prolong, and the intensity of your experience will double. You can also try a vibrating ring that helps you enjoy a gentle pulse while your wife also feels the vibrations. Another way to train your pelvic region to have better control is by practicing deep breathing. Deep breathing also boosts your energy, allows for better cognitive clarity to focus intently on your wife, and it can help you both connect deeper. The risk of not arousing yourself enough is not only for the wife. Men can also struggle to enjoy sex if they didn't arouse themselves enough to maintain an erection long enough for an intense experience. Husbands should avoid certain depressants like alcohol. Any depressant can stop the hormones from doing their thing in the brain.

Coffee and caffeine are okay, but avoid alcohol when you're looking forward to an exceptional experience. The food we eat can also change our intensity because food alters our biochemistry (Mokhtar, 2012). Protein and healthy fats can increase sex hormones and help you sustain a better erection, and spicy foods are known as aphrodisiacs.

Fruit and animal protein are also good for your sex hormones, but stay away from junk food if you wish to experience optimal bliss during sex. Junk food prevents the hormonal changes you need. Some foods just clog your blood vessels, making it impossible to achieve a sustainable and worthy erection. Other than avoiding foods and alcohol that make you struggle to achieve intense orgasms; you should learn to be adventurous.

Ask your wife to help you with this part. She would have to be gentle, but the testicles have many nerve endings, allowing you to use this for better stimulation during sex. Ask your wife to gently massage your balls while you make love. Some men love it when their wives lick their balls. It's highly sensual, and you should try it if you haven't yet. A hidden pleasure center lies within a scrotum, which is a man's G-spot (Weisman, 2018). The prostate is a non-familiar pleasure center, and it lies about two inches away from the rectum near the scrotum. This gland is so sensitive that it can be stimulated externally. A comfortable way to explore this would be to massage the perineum, which is the area of skin between the testicles and the anus, often called "the taint." Some men will enjoy this method because it stimulates the prostate or G-spot from outside the body.

Using the pad of your finger, gently rub or press on that area as you figure out what feels good. This can be coupled with other sensual strokes, sucks, licks, and toys. You can gently place pressure on it while you orgasm. If the prostate is ever stimulated, you'll barely be able to contain your wildness as this is one of the most intense ways you can enhance your experience as a man. Engaging a man, and making him want more and more, which makes you want more and more, can be done easily with these few tricks. Both of you can enjoy the tricks you learned about the opposite gender, and enjoy as many of them together as you can. Marriage and the sexual intimacy required with it means you should be playing together. Don't place limits on anything unless it turns one of you off.

Sometimes, tricks can have the opposite effect. Experiment with a few, and see which ones build the right momentum you both need for ultimate intensity and passion throughout the experience.

Passionate Checklist

The way you arouse each other has endless possibilities. This checklist reminds you of a few ways you can turn the heat up between you. We have listed items the two of you may find useful on our website at the end of the introduction, including adult toys, libido enhancing supplements for women, and more.

- Leave love notes or unexpected surprises for your spouse to find.
- Share numerous deep, passionate, and intense kisses throughout the day.
- Lighten your partner's load so they can focus on you.
- Grind and rub yourself against your partner when you hug them.
- Do something sweet and thoughtful to open the emotional intimacy before the passion ignites.
- Buy your spouse something they mentioned needing in passing.
- Relax your spouse with a massage.
- Bathe or shower together.
- Call your spouse just to flirt with them in a sexy way.
- Husbands, remember to check-in with your wives to make sure she's having orgasms.
- Wives, see what you can do to help your husbands experience multiple orgasms for the first time. It's a gift women have but men want.

Chapter 7:

I'm Not Arguing About the Kids!

You Handle it Then!

Married life can be a blissful journey, and kids are miniature versions of ourselves combined, but there can also be some challenges along the way. As much as you and your spouse are passionately in love with each other, parenting can quickly drive a wedge in all that's good in marriage unless you work as a team. Husbands and wives come from different homes, and they can be expected to think about parenting in different ways. However, allowing your parenting skills to come between you can cause marital problems that can even undo all the work you've done in this book so far. Marriage will be an uphill battle of lost passion, trust, and support if you're both trying to go in different directions. To have a happy marriage, and kids who add to the contentment of the home, you both need to work toward mutual parenting.

A Family Spiral

Parenting comes with endless joys and proud moments, but it also comes with a few complicated habits. You're both unique in all your ways, and you both believe that a parent should be like this or that. One of you might be a permissive type of parent, and the other one might be a disciplinarian parent. The former type of parent prefers to allow the children to spread their wings and learn lessons for themselves, whereas the latter parent prefers strict discipline and punishment. The parenting type you both choose is not wrong or right unless you're using different types. Children are fallible little humans, and they require guidance from their parents. It's confusing for them to have you allow them to talk to you as they wish while your spouse demands respect. What are the kids supposed to think?

What happens in a home where nothing is consistent between the parents and children is that the family divides. The family as a whole disintegrates into divisions where children prefer one parent to the other. Children treat the permissive parent like a friend, and they learn to resent the parent who acts as the authority. Please remember this, married parents should not, under any circumstance, disagree on how to parent the kids in front of their children. These disagreements need to become a compromise on which you can both agree. Children will always try to pick a favorite parent to run to when the other parent says no. This also causes problems between you and your spouse if you believe a child should be allowed to do something but your partner says otherwise. Suddenly, the children become a mechanism to undermine each other as parents.

"Why would Sam run to me if he thought you were a great dad?" "Why would Jessica be afraid to ask you if you weren't so scary?" The kids become a reason for spouses to argue and undermine each other without giving it a second thought. Communication problems set in as kids learn to lose respect for one parent while they know the other parent gives them what they want. You both can forget about the intimacy married couples need when you're constantly mad at each other for parenting the wrong way. Moreover, kids become so confused that they can suffer from anxiety because they don't know what to expect in the home anymore. The greatest tool for parents to raise kids as a team, so the entire family can thrive, is to provide consistency. No child can live without consistency. Remember that your children are highly impressionable.

You are both their first teachers in this world. Wouldn't it be better to raise them as a single unit, so they can become their greatest selves while your marriage retains sanity and passion? Ask yourselves what you wish to see in your children, and then pay attention to why you parent differently. Just as your children learn everything from you, your parents also taught you how to behave and how to relate to your children. According to psychologist Lisa Firestone, it's very likely we become our parents when we have children (Firestone, 2015). We tend to imitate some of the methods we saw in our parents. You may find yourselves reacting in strange ways when a child spills milk all over the floor. Suddenly, you say, "Why the heck did you do that?" Deep in your mind, you know why your child did it. It was an accident, but your reaction could be an imitation of what you consistently heard from your parents.

Perhaps your spouse thinks this behavior calls for a timeout, but you may wonder if your child can really be punished for an accident? Both your upbringings affect the way you decide to parent, and it often comes out of nowhere. Sometimes, we under or overreact because of how we were raised. Maybe your parents were iron fist punishers, and that's why you chose to be a permissive parent. You're trying to compensate for the irresponsible parenting you encountered by allowing your kids too much freedom. This is still a distorted reaction from us as parents, and it swings way too far in the opposite direction. Other times, we can also project the way our parents saw us onto our kids, even when there's no truth to it. Your mom always called you a bad kid, so you may project this onto your child, thinking all kids must be bad.

The same goes for incapable, stupid, wild, or uncontrollable. Your kids become what your parents saw in you, and you stop seeing them as unique individuals. Our kids are extensions of us, but we should only offer consistent structure and guidance. We should never allow our expectations to be tainted by our childhood. Another way either of you may be unloading your childhood in your parenting today is when you try to recreate a childhood you loved. Unfortunately, this doesn't always work. Children of today are different. They have different interests, skills, and opportunities. Just because you loved playing a musical instrument, doesn't mean your son will. We cannot recreate the dynamics of our childhoods, even if we had a great life. Children need to be unique and independent. They need to be themselves. As parents, you may also be unaware of showing some jealousy toward your children. This could've developed in your younger years.

A way it could've come about was if your parents weren't too involved in your life, so your thinking could be, why should you be involved in your children's lives? Or, you could be jealous that your mom wasn't that great toward you, but your wife is a great mother toward your kids, and that makes you jealous of your children. You may find it hard to accept that your children need and love you because no one showed you this before. Automatic defenses or distortions can cloud your parenting. We sometimes also carry triggers with us into our family life. There were hot triggers that caused your parents to blow up, and you may tend to lose your cool as soon as your children behave the same way. It's a subconscious trigger that ignites a reaction before you can even think about it. The final reason why we may parent as we do is that our inner critics have maintained free rein during our childhood.

Our parents have a lot to do with why our inner critics say the things they do, but we can also reinforce our habits in adulthood. We don't think we're good parents, even if no one ever said it. We think we'll raise children to work as cashiers because it's how we earned a living as young adults. We think our children won't make it to college because it runs in the family. That's the problem with the inner critic. It's normally the voice of anything other than reason. It's the voice that belongs to people, parents, friends, and teachers in childhood who had wild expectations of us. This voice amplifies our concerns and insecurities, not knowing that they mostly belong to society. Society has nothing to do with your family today. You and your spouse will raise your children. Only the two of you can design the future they deserve, and by doing it as a team, you can also create a peaceful and loving family environment that doesn't destroy your marriage.

Neither of you should just rely on the methods your parents used to raise you. Those methods need to be re-evaluated for what you want to cultivate in your children. You should put all self-doubts aside, and stand shoulder-to-shoulder in parenting.

A Singular Unit

Whether you believe that kids should be seen and not heard, or you want your kids to make life interesting wherever you go, the two of you should unite as a single force to provide structure and discipline. These are two key components of how your kids will mature into well-rounded and adjusted adults. According to parenting experts who conducted a review of research regarding discipline, kids need it (Lee, 2020). Kids can't become their best selves, and the family can't be a peaceful state if discipline doesn't exist. This is one of the main factors parents need to address as a team. Being on the same page is how you both address issues with your children to provide stability and consistency for them. Disciplining children is as potent for their health and well-being as nutritious food. Children won't have the tools they need in life if parents can't stand together and teach them right from wrong.

Children learn to navigate relationships with other people through your parenting. They adopt self-discipline when they can recognize right from wrong. They have respect for others, and they have no trouble cooperating in team efforts, which makes them prone to have better romantic relationships themselves. Believe it or not, children are happier in a structured home because they know what can be expected of them. They know that certain actions lead to specific reactions, and they can feel reassured that good behaviors lead to great opportunities. People have the wrong idea of discipline. It has nothing to do with teaching your children what they can and can't do. It's about teaching them to choose the right behavior, knowing that wrongs lead to natural consequences and rights lead to opportunities. Discipline is about teaching a child to regulate their own behavior so you don't have to yell at them or argue with your spouse.

Kids gather tools to prevent impulsive behaviors, so they can face challenges with greater ease. They learn to think before they act. Parents also teach their children about conflict resolution, which is an undeniably priceless skill. A child becomes capable of regulating their emotions, and they can develop a stronger relationship with both parents, especially if you're both on the same track. The boundaries and punishments should be set by parents as a team. You should both agree on what you'll allow, and what won't fly in the home. Consequences should also be established and agreed upon by both of you. The only thing that matters here is that you both work as one to establish a list of boundaries you won't tolerate. There should be positive and negative consequences for the behaviors you want to encourage or won't allow.

Making a list together is a bonding exercise for parents, too. Remember to use effective communication skills to listen and say your opinion without getting into a tussle. Then, you need to commit to parenting together. Both parents must enforce the boundaries in the home. Children will learn responsibility, confidence, self-sufficiency, and decision-making skills if you remain consistent.

Changing the Dynamics

We believe the natural order of parenting is a team effort. If one spouse feels that the majority of parenting responsibilities fall on them, resentment and a whole host of other negative feelings will creep in between the two of you. This is certainly not what anyone aims for in their marriage. Parenting will teach you so much about yourself if you're willing to pay attention. In our relationship, even though we had time to prepare and discuss over the years about what type of parents we intended to be and what type of family we wanted to raise, we had so many reality checks when our first child arrived, which led us down a divided road. One spouse just lost their mother and suffered another traumatic experience right before our firstborn arrived. They didn't realize it, but they spiraled into a depressive state.

When our firstborn was around six months, it was evident that the depressed spouse checked out of parenting and left it up to the other spouse for a while. After two years of not truly being involved in parenting, but just being around, separation was almost inevitable, especially when our second child was on the way and no change was happening. What helped us rebound was that the distant spouse had to either choose between dealing with the thought of losing their new family through divorce, or they had to get more involved with the day-to-day details of being a parent. There should be one thing on which the two of you agree. The main team decision is that you'll never argue about how to discipline the kids in front of them. The kids should know, loud and clear, that their discipline isn't negotiable by running to one parent.

Kids should know that you'll stand together to address the issues or concerns that came about because of them. Keep in mind that the more time you spend on the two of you arguing about discipline, the less time and energy you both have to deal with the unwanted behavior of your children. The two of you should find a common ground on which to stand. You should explore and share the reasons why you disagree on the discipline, which you've both done effectively in the previous section. Establishing a safe word to use between you and your spouse can also prevent things from blowing up before you deal with the issue. Plan a safe word you can use when one parent feels like they need to discuss the outcome first. Most problems between kids don't have to be solved immediately, especially when a child is throwing a tantrum for dropping their juice box on the floor.

Many parents also love turning to the "good cop, bad cop" game. Please don't. Neither of you should be vying for your children's affection over your partner. Neither of you should make your children choose a preferred parent. You're either both bad or good cops because your children should see you as a single mind. Once both parents agree on what comes next, both of you need to stick to it. Don't give in to children's tantrums and bad behaviors in the hopes of keeping them quiet. This automatically makes you the good cop against your spouse again. Trust us, giving up to make children behave better doesn't work. Both of you should have a discipline plan in place before war breaks out between kids and whatever or whoever upset them. The boundaries and consequences of breaking the boundaries should be effectively communicated to your children as a team.

Both of you should be clearly explaining the same story, even if you sound like broken records at first. When designing your behavioral plan as a single front, be honest with your spouse about your strengths and weaknesses, too. Knowing where you're strong and weak can benefit the entire family when problems need to be solved. Your family will become more balanced as you and your spouse focus on using your strengths to coach the children to self-control. Your marriage will also be better off in the long run. Having conversations about your strengths and weaknesses as a married couple will help you both realize that there may be times mom must take the lead, and there might be times dad needs to lead in areas mom might not be as strong. You can discuss hypothetical scenarios to determine whether mom or dad is better suited to handle the discipline for a specific topic.

The two of you should discuss different situations before they arise. Choosing to speak from a stance of your strengths will also help you be more assertive and consistent, and it can gain more respect from a child if their parent can relate to the issue somehow. Both of you should discuss the matter beforehand to agree on what the potential consequences of a child's actions should be, but some discussions are better suited for one parent, depending on their strengths. An example scenario might be for dad to lead the discipline if his son speaks rudely to adults. Dad feels that respect is a critical facet of social interactions, and it can't be dismissed for whatever reason. The dad could relate to the child by sharing his workplace dynamics. He would be fired if he were to speak to his boss without respect. This would change the home dynamics because there wouldn't be money for all the videogames his son enjoys so much. The dad might feel like he can be more assertive in this case, and the mom can simply offer support as the dad reminds his son of the consequences of being rude to adults. In this case, the consequence might be to lose his videogame privileges. Mom might feel her strength is to take the lead when her son was caught lying again. She might be able to connect deeper with his emotional reasons for thinking lies are okay. Kids often lie because they're afraid to speak the truth, so mom can hand down a suitable consequence after considering the emotional implications of her son's habit. The child needs to be more comfortable to be open with his parents, and his mom might believe that she can encourage him to be more open about his feelings.

The child with a lying habit still needs discipline, but mom can make him write apology notes for his lies. Let's take another example where you catch a child stealing. Perhaps dad feels strongly that he can solve this issue and discipline his daughter. He may feel like this issue requires a strength he possesses by being a little authoritative. His daughter denies her wrongdoings, and he can remind her that theft also hurts someone, breaking a boundary as much as rudeness. The two of you might choose to enforce a sense of responsibility in your daughter, which deters her from stealing again. However, dad can enforce this as mom offers support again. Mom might choose to be the frontrunner with tantrums again. Tantrums are also emotional, so a woman may feel more comfortable leading the discipline on the issue. Women relate easier to emotional things, and men relate better to rational solutions.

A tantrum is a toddler's way of expressing emotions when they don't know another way. Mom may feel that a timeout could work in this case because it allows the child to calm down while being away from any triggers. So, she would take the lead. Mom and dad show a united front and won't give their toddler attention until she calms down. Both parents can be present for these scenarios, but there are some scenarios that require a man or woman's innate strengths. Potty training is also a discipline, and it may be best if mom teaches her daughters and dad teaches his sons. Toddlers know nothing about our physiology, and having the same gender parent face this issue with them is better to help them understand it faster. However, the more pressing scenario is when you catch a child masturbating for the first time. As it was said before, the two of you should discuss beforehand how you all want to handle the situation before it comes up.

Decide who is better suited to tackle this in the moment, or if it's something you both want to address. Mom could best tell her daughter about her body, and dad can definitely explain things to his son in a relatable way. The two of you may decide that you both want to chime in to give them a balanced viewpoint. This is why effective planning and communication between spouses goes a long way for the betterment of your entire family unit. Whether you choose to discipline certain behaviors as an equal team, or you choose specific parents to lead on certain issues, you should still plan everything before the problem arises. Go through various scenarios to discuss how you both can manage the parenting journey better as a single unit.

Team Discipline Checklist

As a parenting team, you can use this checklist to make your family life a lot smoother and happier.

- Always talk about disagreements away from the kids. Never allow kids to see their parents disagree or get into an argument.

- Be willing to compromise with your spouse to find common ground. There has to be an outcome both of you can accept.

- Actively listen to your spouse's reasoning before making a decision. Remember that they were raised in a home where their parenting was the norm.

- Always talk about parenting and discipline when you're both in a good, calm state of mind. Effective communication must be used in every part of your marriage, including parenting.

- Model the team effort in everything you do in front of the kids. They'll learn to adopt your values, beliefs, and behaviors, so be a good example as parents.

- Make a list of five boundaries that broadly cover the basics of social interaction, and these will be the boundaries you both agree to discipline your children with if they cross the line. Do the same with consequences.

Chapter 8:

Loving Parents, Enjoyable Kids.

Creating a strong family bond that will last doesn't only come from team parenting in discipline. A happy marriage relies on the connectedness of all of your family members. It depends on how you all get along, and how much time you spend together. Kids are like clay being molded in our hands, and we can't expect our home to be a blissful state unless we consider all the ways our hands shape our children. Kids need parents to show them right from wrong, but they also need us to be their pillars of strength, their coaches who cheer them on, and their loving parents who teach them what positive emotions look like. Unhappy kids equal an unhappy home and marriage, so you both need to understand what can go wrong and how to change the dynamics of your family for now and in the future.

An Unavoidable Truth

Before trying to understand the inner workings of a miniature you, you must both evaluate the way you feel about parenting because it can expose so many truths and reality checks. The way parenting has affected both of you mentally and physically can be seen in your daily interactions with your children. It might not be clear at first, especially if you haven't asked yourself the toughest question parents face. We will ask you a question many parents won't like. It will make you uncomfortable, but it's necessary. What was the reason you had children? Did you have children by accident, or was the pregnancy planned? The reason we ask this question is that your outlook and feelings surrounding how your children came to be has a major impact on how you raise them and how deep your bond will grow with them.

It needs to be said, just because you're a parent, it doesn't automatically mean your ability to love, nurture, care for, or teach your children is there. Most importantly, it's not a given that because you have children, you're able to prioritize their needs before yours. We experienced this first-hand from our parents growing up, and we've seen this clearly over the last 12 years as foster parents. To build a stronger bond with your children, you'll need to look within to make sure you're sharing balanced interactions with your kiddos. If either of you is a parent who feels you had your children before you were ready, and you were thrust into parenthood, you may not even realize it, but your interactions with them may come across as though they're a bother to you, or they're a nagging sore.

The truth doesn't change the fact that you love them deeply, but it changes the way you parent. If you are parents like us, who had to go through the experience of many ups and downs to overcome infertility, having numerous in-vitro fertilization (IVF) treatments to have our family, you could be unintentionally way too lenient and permissive. You may lack the necessary structure and discipline your children need because it wasn't easy having them. We had to make sure we didn't fall prey to this behavior. This is just a check-in with you to see if, as a parent, you're searching within to keep a balance in your daily life with your kids, and that you're not imprinting on them negatively while being totally unaware of your behavior as a parent. The focus is often placed on children, but parents can also behave in ways that impact their children negatively.

Both examples are subtle, and many parents won't even notice how they feel toward their children unless they evaluate themselves. The first example seems like outright neglect, and in some way, it is, but the parent may not even realize it. The second example, if we would have approached our children that way, it would also be neglectful. As parents, we should always be fully aware of the impact we have on our kids when we do or say something. We also should recognize what influence we have when we say and do nothing. Children need an emotional connection with us. They need to establish an emotionally intimate bond with their parents. If you found the first question hard, consider whether you want your children to be close to you, or whether you want them to be distant and underdeveloped. Both of you must realize that your parenting methods can also impact the way your children connect with you.

Emotional neglect can subtly underlie interactions with our children, and many parents don't even notice it. Children have emotional needs, and a parent's inability to adequately address their emotional needs, whether intentional or not, is what's called emotional neglect. A child's emotions might seem unconventional and dysfunctional, but their emotions are real nonetheless. Emotional neglect is not to be mistaken for intentional emotional abuse. It's when parents unintentionally disregard the feelings of their child when they think children don't understand or have big feelings. Kids don't know how to manage their emotions. They need their parents to be the supportive and listening adult who guides them through the battlefield of scary feelings. Sometimes, their feelings aren't as scary as they think, but they've never faced them before, so fear sets in, which is a big emotion in itself, even for adults.

The two of you may be giving love and discipline, but you might be dismissing feelings. The impact of emotional neglect can be so subtle that parents can easily overlook it. They may never notice how they influenced their children, much like how our parents subconsciously influenced us. Neither of you are bad parents. No parent who wishes to improve their relationship with their children is a bad parent. Most of the time, they just haven't learned how to improve their relationships with their kids yet. The impact on emotionally neglected children can vary from subtle to extreme, but they all leave a lasting scar (Holland, 2019). Children may show signs of apathy as they lose interest in activities they once enjoyed. They could become hyperactive or aggressive, which only makes the family dynamic harder to turn peaceful.

Kids can become withdrawn socially and developmentally. Emotionally neglected children can start shunning intimacy and closeness with friends and family. It's possible for their self-esteem to plunge to new lows, and they could find it hard to thrive in school and social circles. Anxiety and depression could become familiar to your children, and they may even entertain the thought of substance abuse. These kids turn into adults who don't have the vital skills needed to thrive in the world. Perhaps you notice how your childhood was void of emotional support, and this may allow you to see some of the adult after-effects of growing up without emotional support. The consequences in adulthood come in the form of post-traumatic stress disorder (PTSD), depression, anxiety, emotional unavailability, and poor self-discipline.

Adults might also experience a failure to be intimate with their partners, children, and friends. They may feel empty, unwanted, and not good enough. They may suffer from guilt, shame, aggression, and mistrust. These people will always see someone unworthy in the mirror. They only see flaws, and they can even suffer from eating disorders. The biggest risk of having no emotional recognition in childhood is that you grow up to parent your children the same way. You may never have known how important your emotions were, and this ripples through your life. Do you really want your children to feel like they aren't allowed to have emotions? Most parents aim to be the best for their children. Parents don't have children with the intention of neglecting them as those little bundles of joy enter the home, but it happens. The reasons why parents emotionally neglect their children can also range.

The most obvious reason is that they grew up without understanding the relevance of their emotions. They have a lack of emotional fulfillment in their own lives, and they might be uneducated about good parenting skills. Mental health disorders and substance abuse also cause emotional neglect toward children, but the most subtle reason you may neglect your children is that you resent them. You didn't feel ready to have kids, but guess what? They're here now. Whether you weren't ready, or you hope to simply improve your relationship even more with your children, it's time to start taking note of their feelings. Even if a child approaches you with the silliest issue, listen to them so they know how those big emotions mean something. It makes them precious humans.

The next time your child wants to tell you how the new preschool classmate shows his sneakers off like some superstar, ask your child how it makes them feel. When your teenage daughter tells you about her friend who gossiped behind her back, ask her to share her feelings with you. When a toddler gets frustrated for not building the tallest Lego tower, remind him that you know how it feels to want something and not get it. Then, encourage him to try again. It doesn't matter how silly their feelings seem to you. These emotions are new and unfamiliar to your children. As a mom or dad, both of you need to connect emotionally with your children. Both of you require that intimate bond with your kids to ensure a peaceful, happy, and connected home.

Precious Time

Time must be the most valuable commodity in the universe. It can't be altered or skipped, but it can fly by. The most precious gift you can ever share with your spouse, family as a whole, or a child who needs to connect deeper with you, is time. Children don't remember the allowance they spent, but they recall the moments they shared with friends, parents, and siblings. Experiences require an investment of time, but these are the events that instill memories. It's also become a challenge nowadays because parents have the benefit of technology to keep their children busy. Instead of spending time with their children as a family, they give them smartphones and tablets to keep them busy. Kids are losing their ability to develop social skills because these traits aren't collected on social media.

In fact, social media burdens our kids with low self-esteem and social awkwardness. The digital era never brought us simpler ways to connect with the people we love and care about. It also brought a devolution that breaks our social needs as humans, and this is happening to children daily. A study published in *Plos One* revealed the differences between real social interactions and virtual interactions to compare the benefits to our health (Lin et al., 2019). Ironically, health and fitness data were collected with digital trackers, but the results leaned profoundly toward the participants who had strong social circles beyond the digital world. People with large and strong social networks proved to be mentally and physically healthier than those who only relied on virtual relationships.

If you want a strong family bond that lasts a lifetime, then you need to be the parents who spend real time with your children, allowing them to emotionally connect with you. Spending time as a deeply connected family leads to a meaningful life for children and parents. We would also like to remind parents that they must be careful to evenly spread their attention and time between the kids, irrespective of their gender and preferences. Your sons and daughters should enjoy equal benefits from both of you, including time and energy. It could be easy for one parent to be excited about one child's interests or activities over the other child. Trust and believe your children will notice your preferences as a parent, and it can cause a child to be jealous, act out behaviorally, become insecure, and learn poor self-discipline because they don't get enough attention from you.

Perhaps dad loves football, and his son is now playing the sport. He may be spending more time with his son surrounding the sport, and he could be investing time and energy as a coach and mentor. However, this dad's daughter could be a cheerleader or dancer, and he doesn't have much interest in these activities, so he doesn't spend time with her. The dad doesn't talk to her or help her with practice, but she still feels excited about her interests. Now, she simply feels emotionally neglected because her dad focuses too much on football. She may end up resenting her brother, dad, and maybe herself. The parenting relationship is like any other connection where you require balance. According to behavioral specialist Doctor Todd Thatcher, a family needs to spend time together to bond so they can benefit in numerous ways (Thatcher, 2020).

Children learn the value of communication skills and education, helping them improve their academic performance. It boosts their self-confidence to know how much they're appreciated by their family, and it reduces stress when they learn that it's safe to confide in family members. Children learn to become flexible and resilient. They know they belong somewhere in this world, and this knowledge allows them to face challenges without fear. Children feel like they have a purpose in this world when their parents are set on spending time with them. Their mental health improves, and they have a reduced risk of suffering from depression or anxiety. They benefit from being physically present in the only moment that matters with the people they love. This is how memories are created, and these memories give them something to hold onto when the tides rise higher.

Children who spend time with their parents and families are also at a lower risk of developing behavioral problems. As parents give them positive attention in return for positive behavior, they learn to understand that we get what we give. Children start desiring improved behavior because it leads to the emotional intimacy they need. Kids know they can express themselves when their parents are prepared to listen without needing to rush off to the next task of the day. Children are better able to make positive decisions and bring their problems to you if you open your time and energy to their needs. Spending time as a family, and providing the support and value each of you requires, helps children develop problem-solving and conflict resolution skills. Once they know their opinions are taken seriously, they start looking for solutions to challenges they face, increasing their ability to cope with obstacles.

Children learn to have constructive conversations, even when their opinions differ from yours and other people. They become motivated to push forward in life, and their physical health improves, too. Families who sit down for dinner together are more easily capable of teaching their kids to eat right. Encouraging kids to play sports and games together can improve their fitness as well. Spending time with family can boost your brain, heart, hormonal, and immune health, and it can lead to better longevity. Who doesn't want their children to grow old? The happier, healthier, and more resilient children grow up to be, the longer they live. Family time has to be a priority to ensure healthy individuals connect with the deepest bonds a family can experience. The cherry on top is that your children will grow up to be emotionally stable and supportive parents who connect deeply with their children and spouses.

The kind of connection you want with your spouse is the same type of bond everyone dreams about. Make it simple for your children by designing a childhood where they can grow into loving parents and spouses themselves. Keep in mind that it starts with setting an example. Your children will only mirror what they consistently see from you. Show them loving parents, and they'll share the love and be loving as children. It's important that your children get both sides of you, fun and discipline. Balance is truly the key to a strong, unbreakable family bond. Both parents should equally want to create fun activities and plan outings for their family that will produce wonderful memories for years to come. Creating family bonding time together will also greatly benefit the two of you as spouses because it's more time you're spending together, doing something fun and exciting.

This is what life should truly be about, spending time with your family and sharing memories that last a lifetime. It's not just about doing the bare minimum to get by. The same goes for the relationship between you and your spouse. If you say "life is too busy" or "I'm too busy for family time," we say untangle yourself and get unbusy to make time. Figure out ways to get more rest, but family time is non-negotiable. Take a look at everyone's schedule, and figure out ways to prioritize your family time. No one knows their exit date from this world, so you should take advantage of every moment of each day to show those whom you're closest to and whom you love the most, just how much they mean to you. To create a deeper bond for your family, mom and dad need to create bonding moments and opportunities. This is so important, and not just for the kids, but for you both as parents as well.

Our children look forward to family nights. They have a say in what family night will be and what we'll do, and we shake it up constantly unless they want it to stay the same. As parents, you need to offer these opportunities as consistently as you discipline your kids. Consistency is a crucial part of every parenting responsibility and experience. Consistency is the key to letting the kids know how you feel every moment of every day. Family nights will allow you all to have fun and enjoy each other as a family. You're probably familiar with the famous quote: "A family that plays together stays together." And what matters is that both of you remain consistent, even when there are bad days. You must allow your children to see the good and bad days because this is how they learn to handle the ups and downs of life.

If you show them stress, anger, anxiety, frustration, and fear most of the time, this is what they learn and how they react to stressful situations when they arise. It becomes a vicious cycle when your kids mimic you in a bad way because you both influence each other's moods, too. We joke all the time about our five-year-old daughter because she's such a little drama queen, but we're careful never to call her one though. She's completely over the top about the littlest things, but we can see from where she gets it. She gets some of her behavioral responses from her dad because sometimes, he reacts the same way, especially if he's joking and because she's young, she can't tell the difference. The great thing is that her dad realized how she was mimicking his behavior, and he's working on modeling better behavior for her now.

Our daughter is also learning to manage her inner diva because she's seeing how she should react from us as parents. She has that security of knowing we're paying attention to her during our family bonding nights. She has the freedom to express herself in a way that doesn't negatively affect anyone else's emotions. What we've turned into a habit in our family is to schedule regular family nights. We had to move a few things around to make the time our family needed to unify, but we did it. We call it the playbook, but this is the schedule that reminds us of family nights and days. Create your own playbook as a couple, and include the kids in the plans. Perhaps you can dedicate one night weekly to a family night, and you can have weekends where Saturday or Sunday is family time. Include a little bit of everything in your playbook so each family member feels appreciated and loved for their unique interests.

Try to avoid activities that make any family member uncomfortable, such as bungee jumping on Saturday when your son is terrified of heights. The two of you, and your children, should each choose activities that promote your interests and that the family can enjoy together. Mom and dad can each have time alone with children, too, but make sure neither of you is spending more time or energy on one child over another. Equal time and effort should be shared because it's the foundation of connecting as a whole family.

The Playbook Checklist

These are some ideas we find enjoyable as a family. You can use inspiration from this playbook list to design yours.

- Take the entire family for a pizza night at a restaurant.

- Make dinner as a family. Allow the kids to help mix ingredients while mom or dad handles the hot stove. Try a new recipe everyone chooses from a book or website. Allow each person in the kitchen to have equal responsibilities.

- Have a board game night. There's a board game for just about anything and any age group. Some popular ideas include *Beat the Parents*, *Monopoly*, *Exploding Kittens*, *Clue*, and *Spot It*. You can also try *Spontuneous*, which encourages no talent at all, and it's a laugh-a-minute game. *Mouse Trap* is a great board game to teach kids about teamwork, and *Jumanji* is great for bigger kids. You can also go for *Family Charades* for more laughs, or you can stick to *Jenga*, which encourages problem-solving.

- Add hide and seek to your playbook, and it can be played inside or outside.

- Have a hot cocoa and chocolate day. Make it a chocolate theme day and create a hot cocoa bar with different flavors and toppings.

- You can add a park day where you spend the day playing games and family sports in the park. Outdoor activities are great for weekend family time.

- You can also have an arts and crafts day. Kids love creating stuff, and doing arts and crafts allows their creative beasts to surface. Creativity is a valuable skill to develop. Have a type of craft in mind for the night. Some ideas are to create a family scrapbook, paint sneakers with fabric paints, decorate pencils, or make masks. The crafts will depend on the age group of your children.

- Nothing says family night quite like the classic movie and popcorn combo. Choose a movie that teaches children a life lesson or one that makes you all fold with laughter. Okay, parents might not enjoy the animated movies, but movie night has to be about what's appropriate for the kids. Who knows? You might enjoy the children's movie anyway. Let the kids choose one if you're brave enough.

- Camp out in the backyard with your kids. Toast some marshmallows, and tell stories around the campfire in your garden.

- Another idea for brave parents is to create a family band night. Unless you have real instruments, it might get loud and crazy. Make sure you won't disturb the neighbors first, but go ahead and bang together on pots and pans.

- Have a dance party for family members only. Choose music appropriate for your children, and boogie the night away.

- Turn your backyard into a paintball arena by filling balloons with child-friendly colored water.

- Create a family fitness night by building a simple obstacle course in your living room or yard, depending on the age groups of your children.

- Have a family science night where you look for appropriate experiments online to test in the kitchen. Parents may need to purchase the items beforehand.

- Be creative, and have fun while experimenting with new ideas.

Conclusion

Marriage started as a union of bliss, passion, and shared dreams, but the two of you learned the truth behind marriage as time passed. Hurdles will be thrown on your track, and some couples simply get bored with each other. They once had the passion and intimacy they desired, but the marriage slowly grew stagnant. They drifted apart, and may not even enjoy each other's company anymore. Other couples have faced more demanding challenges where trust was broken, and they don't know if they can trust each other again. It's easy to hurt someone, whether it happens intentionally or not.

Negative emotions and resentment can simmer between spouses until they question whether their marriage is worth saving. Some couples may believe their marriage is beyond reparation. Other times, marriage takes a steady and subtle decline toward lost communication and a lack of sex. One spouse might still have a flame burning inside of their desires for their partner, but the other spouse moves away from them. Intimacy falls, and they don't know how to communicate with each other. It's not always the physical intimacy that fails. It can also be the emotional intimacy that takes a dip, making way for cohabitation instead of marriage. Suddenly, you both feel like you're cohabiting the space you share.

You might find it hard to feel the way you did about your spouse. Anger, frustration, and constant arguments could be the daily routine. Forgiveness is but another dream between you, for both the spouse who must forgive and the one who must receive it. Sometimes, marriage simply lacks fun and excitement. Either or both spouses can feel like marriage becomes a chore. Perhaps you feel like your spouse can't fulfill your needs anymore, and divorce becomes an option. What challenges marriage beyond these issues is when children are part of your home. Children are amazing, but they can also give their married parents a run for their money. Being in an unhealthy marriage only makes parenting harder, too.

You have to ask yourself whether your marriage is influencing your parenting, or whether the way you parent your children as a couple is destroying your marriage. Everyone wants and deserves a happy, loving marriage. These issues won't be yours anymore now that you both know what needs to happen. You both need to work at improving your communication skills. You both have to up your game to understand why forgiveness is a secret belonging to happily married couples. The two of you must continue to work toward true intimacy, and you both need to put your spouse's needs before your own. They have needs just like you, and you can't expect your spouse to prioritize yours if you aren't willing to do the same.

Marriage has never been a 50/50 partnership. Our experience showed us that marriage requires 100/100 to work well. So, learn to love your spouse for all their imperfections, as well as their needs. The two of you can rekindle the passionate intimacy you desire, emotionally and physically. Don't allow the marriage to go stale again. Keep the flame burning with excitement and new experiences. You know how to spice up your routine so both of you can look at each other through the eyes of love and deep affection again. You can admire each other, and you can find ways to build and sustain trust, irrespective of what brought you to this book. Use the tools of connectedness to deepen your love and passion for each other, and never allow the distractions of a failed world to enter your marriage again.

Be with each other. Be one with each other, and welcome the mutual flourishing as a husband and wife as you try the sexual tricks you learned about. Don't be shy, and go all out to get your husband or wife into the most intense experience you'll ever share. Hot, passionate sex is possible again, and it can follow the most broken marriages once repaired correctly. Once your souls are interconnected as a married couple again, you can turn to your parenting to ensure a team effort so the children can contribute to the family connection. You can work together to create a home that doesn't only promote a happy marriage. It also promotes healthier and happier children.

Your family can be complete so that you can always face and destroy the obstacles in your way. Moreover, the love shared between parents and children and vice versa will make your marriage worth every second you make an effort. Our challenges taught us valuable lessons, and with 25 years of tools under our belts, we hope that you both find the kind of marriage we share today after absorbing our experiences and advice. From both of us to the both of you, we want to remind you that no marriage is unfixable. Every marriage has a path forward if you both make the effort. Love doesn't die. It simply goes dormant until you awaken it again.

References

ABC News. (2010, March 24). *Q&A with Dr. Louann Brizendine, author of "The Male Brain."* ABC News. https://abcnews.go.com/GMA/Books/louann-brizendine-answers-questions/story?id=10184876

Baumgardner, J. (2017, October 23). *Why date night matters.* First Things First. https://firstthings.org/why-date-night-matters/

Baumgardner, J. (2018, July 9). *Couples who play together.* First Things First. https://firstthings.org/couples-who-play-together/

Benson, H. (2016, September 27). *The benefits of monthly date nights for married couples.* Institute for Family Studies. https://ifstudies.org/blog/the-benefits-of-monthly-date-nights-for-married-couples

Bolmont, M., Cacioppo, J. T., & Cacioppo, S. (2014). Love is in the gaze. *Psychological Science, 25*(9), 1748–1756. https://doi.org/10.1177/0956797614539706

Borresen, K. (2019, January 2). *The most common problems that arise after 10 years of marriage.* HuffPost. https://www.huffpost.com/entry/marriage-problems-solutions-10-years_n_5c2a4a80e4b08aaf7a92bcfb

Boston Medical Group. (2018, August 9). *Don't ignore the foreplay.* Boston Medical Group. https://www.bostonmedicalgroup.com/dont-ignore-the-foreplay/

Breen, P. (2019, September 20). *Learning to listen without getting defensive.* Verily. https://verilymag.com/2019/09/how-to-listen-without-getting-defensive-2019

Carter, Z. (2017, June 12). *Three nonverbal behaviors that may damage your marriage.* Psychology Today. https://www.psychologytoday.com/us/blog/clear-communication/201706/three-nonverbal-behaviors-may-damage-your-marriage

Caston, C. (2014, November 3). *3 things men want from their wives.* Marriage365®. https://marriage365.com/blog/3-things-husbands-want-from-their-wife/

Chan, J. (2017, August 16). *The differences between male and female communication style in the workplace.* Loopline Systems. https://www.loopline-systems.com/en/blog-en/the-differences-between-male-and-female-communication-style-in-workplace

Cobb, N. (2013). *Defuse couples conflict with an effective time-out.* Nathan Cobb. https://www.nathancobb.com/couple-conflict.html

Figure One. (n.d.). Pixabay. https://pixabay.com/photos/people-girl-woman-female-sexy-2561600/

Firestone, L. (2015, July 30). *7 ways your childhood affects how you'll parent.* Psychology Today. https://www.psychologytoday.com/us/blog/compassion-matters/201507/7-ways-your-childhood-affects-how-youll-parent

Forrey, J. (2017, May 10). *How differently do men and women communicate?* Care Leader. https://www.careleader.org/differently-men-women-communicate/

Good Therapy. (2013, January 28). *What is intimacy?* Good Therapy. https://www.goodtherapy.org/blog/psychpedia/intimacy

Gordon, K. C., Baucom, D. H., & Snyder, D. K. (2005). Treating couples recovering from infidelity: An integrative approach. *Journal of Clinical Psychology, 61*(11), 1393–1405. https://doi.org/10.1002/jclp.20189

Holland, K. (2019, November 25). *Childhood emotional neglect: What it is, and how it can affect you.* Healthline. https://www.healthline.com/health/mental-health/childhood-emotional-neglect

Lee, K. (2020, October 1). *Surprising reasons why we need to discipline children.* Verywell Family. https://www.verywellfamily.com/surprising-reasons-why-we-need-to-discipline-children-620115#:~:text=In%20fact%2C%20failure%20to%20discipline

Lin, S., Faust, L., Robles-Granda, P., Kajdanowicz, T., & Chawla, N. V. (2019). Social network structure is predictive of health and wellness. *PLOS ONE, 14*(6), e0217264. https://doi.org/10.1371/journal.pone.0217264

Marie Claire. (2020, February 11). *18 tips for a better orgasm.* Marie Claire. https://www.marieclaire.com/sex-love/a162/orgasm-secret/

Marin, V. (2017, April 17). *Do you get distracted during sex? Here's how to focus.* Bustle. https://www.bustle.com/p/do-you-get-distracted-during-sex-heres-how-to-focus-51630#:~:text=Getting%20distracted%20during%20sex%20doesn

Mauer, E. D. (2019, October 18). *Are sexless marriages more common than we think?* The Healthy. https://www.thehealthy.com/family/relationships/are-sexless-marriages-more-common-than-we-think/

McCready, A. (2018, December 31). *When parents disagree on discipline: 8 steps to harmonious parenting.* Positive Parenting Solutions. https://www.positiveparentingsolutions.com/discipline/parents-disagree-on-discipline

Mendez, B., & Hallett, K. (2015, April 2). *5 tips to deepen your sexual connection with your partner.* Mind Body Green.

https://www.mindbodygreen.com/0-18126/5-tips-to-deepen-your-sexual-connection-with-your-partner.html

Men's XP. (2012, March 15). *The importance of foreplay*. Men's XP. https://www.mensxp.com/dating/dating-tips/6364-the-importance-of-foreplay.html

Moali, N. (2020, July 28). *The key to great sex in long-term relationships with Dr. Stephen Snyder*. Sexology Podcast. https://sexologypodcast.com/2020/07/28/ep187-the-key-to-great-sex-in-long-term-relationships-with-dr-stephen-snyder/

Mokhtar, N. A. (2012, June 10). *Hormones help in sex*. Primanora. https://www.primanora.com/wp-content/uploads/2016/12/Hormones-help-in-sex.pdf

Morin, A. (2019a, June 24). *How to avoid common parenting blunders*. Verywell Family. https://www.verywellfamily.com/the-4-biggest-discipline-mistakes-parents-make-1094832

Morin, A. (2019b, August 14). *8 parenting skills that promote the most effective discipline*. Verywell Family. https://www.verywellfamily.com/parenting-skills-effective-discipline-1094835

Muehlhoff, T. (2011, January 18). *Building a strong communication climate*. Family Life®. https://www.familylife.com/podcast/familylife-today/building-a-strong-communication-climate/

Nittrouer, C. L., Hebl, M. R., Ashburn-Nardo, L., Trump-Steele, R. C. E., Lane, D. M., & Valian, V. (2017). Gender disparities in colloquium speakers at top universities. *Proceedings of the National Academy of Sciences, 115*(1), 104–108. https://doi.org/10.1073/pnas.1708414115

Otiende, N. (2013, December 17). *8 things your husband can't get enough of (and how to give them!)*. Intentional Today. https://intentionaltoday.com/8-things-your-husband-cant-get-enough-of-4/

Otiende, N. (2019, September 24). *9 things women want from their husbands for a happy marriage*. Intentional Today. https://intentionaltoday.com/things-women-want-from-their-husbands/

Parker, W. (2020, February 4). *7 ways men can grow intimacy in marriage*. Verywell Mind. https://www.verywellmind.com/men-growing-intimacy-in-marriage-1270945

Rankin, K. (2019, December 12). *The 10 things that sexually connected couples do*. Keeley Rankin - Sex & Relationship Coach. https://keeleyrankin.com/ways-couples-stay-sexually-connected/

Santos-Longhurst, A. (2018, July 10). *16 reasons to kiss*. Healthline. https://www.healthline.com/health/benefits-of-kissing

Shpancer, N. (2015, February 3). *Why we can't stay focused during sex, and why it matters*. Psychology Today. https://www.psychologytoday.com/us/blog/insight-therapy/201502/why-we-cant-stay-focused-during-sex-and-why-it-matters

Smith, L. (2018, February 16). *8 ways men and women communicate differently*. A Conscious Rethink. https://www.aconsciousrethink.com/7282/men-women-communicate-differently/

Smith, S. (2015, September 23). *The significance and importance of forgiveness in a marriage*. Marriage Advice - Expert Marriage Tips & Advice. https://www.marriage.com/advice/forgiveness/the-importance-of-forgiveness-in-a-marriage/

Smith, S., & Welch, A. (2018, January 10). *6 tips to connect emotionally during sex*. Marriage. https://www.marriage.com/advice/physical-intimacy/6-ways-to-connect-during-sex/

Souders, B. (2019, August 20). *The importance of forgiveness in marriage and relationships.* Positive Psychology. https://positivepsychology.com/forgiveness-marriage-relationships/

Stritof, S. (2003, December 14). *Forgiveness and letting go in your marriage.* Verywell Mind; https://www.verywellmind.com/forgiveness-and-letting-go-in-marriage-2300611

Thatcher, T. (2020, March 17). *The top ten benefits of spending time with family.* Highland Springs. https://highlandspringsclinic.org/blog/the-top-ten-benefits-of-spending-time-with-family/

The Doctors Staff. (2012, June 5). *Foreplay.* The Doctors. https://www.thedoctorstv.com/articles/442-foreplay#:~:text=Dr.

Weisman, C. (2018, April 25). *8 ways to have stronger, more pleasurable orgasms.* Fatherly. https://www.fatherly.com/love-money/ways-men-stronger-pleasurable-orgasms-sex/

Wikipedia. (2021, February 21). *Physical intimacy.* Wikipedia. https://en.wikipedia.org/wiki/Physical_intimacy

www.ingramcontent.com/pod-product-compliance
Lightning Source LLC
Chambersburg PA
CBHW020911080526
44589CB00011B/545